My Journey
THROUGH THE
UNITED STATES

8 DOLLARS AND NO DREAM

My *Journey* through the UNITED STATES

8 DOLLARS AND NO DREAM

DR. VED V. GOSSAIN

Copyright © 2022 Dr. Ved V. Gossain.

All rights reserved. No part of this book may be reproduced in any form or by any electronic or mechanical means, including information storage and retrieval systems, without permission in writing from the publisher, except by reviewers, who may quote brief passages in a review.

ISBN: 978-1-957054-48-3 (Paperback Edition)
ISBN: 978-1-957054-49-0 (Hardcover Edition)
ISBN: 978-1-957054-47-6 (E-book Edition)

Book Ordering Information

Phone Number: 315-537-3088 ext 1007
Email: info@theregencypublishers.com
Global Summit House
www.globalsummithouse.com

Printed in the United States of America

DEDICATED TO THE MEMORY OF
DR. VEENA VIRMANI GOSSAIN

(1942-1978)
Ved V. GOSSAIN MD, FRCP ©, MACP, FACE
Swartz Professor of Medicine and Chief
Division of Endocrinology (Emeritus)
Michigan State University
East Lansing Michigan. U.S.A.

REVIEWS

1. "A Chronicle of life that is so deserving of chronicling. It is a primer on how to battle the accident of birth and the misfortunes of life with love, perseverance, and grit. The book makes for a riveting read and many immigrants will see parallels in their own lives

   Satish Udpa.
   University distinguished Professor of
   Electrical and Computer engineering
   former acting president
   Michigan State University .
   East Lansing Michigan. USA .

2. My Journey Through the United States: Eight Dollars and No Dream is a book of surprises, both painful and exciting. It recounts the inspiring story of a young Indian doctor, as he unfolds a new life in America to become a highly successful academic physician and an exemplary husband and parent. But, as he retires, Dr. Gossain wonders if life would have been better, had they stayed back in India. He asks if this lifelong change was worth it and finds the answer in the ancient wisdom of the Bhagavad Gita. It's worth reading the book just to learn his solution—one that can guide us all."

   Robert C. Smith, MD, MACP
   University Distinguished Professor
   Emeritus of Medicine and Psychiatry
   Michigan State University, College of Human Medicine

3. By structuring his book using the "stages of an immigrant" the author frames his journey in a very accessible way. The story he tells of his intellectual and personal journey is intensely relatable centered on the primacy of worthwhile work and the love of family.

   Dianne Wagner.MD
   Senior Associate Dean, college of Human Medicine
   Michigan State University.
   East Lansing, Michigan ,USA.

4. This is a fascinating story of a young physician from India ,who had no intentions of settling in the USA ,but stayed. Despite some misfortunes and many obstacles along the way, he went on to have a highly successful professional career. Everyone, especially immigrants, their children and potential immigrants will learn something from his experience and that is what makes this book worth reading

   R.K Pandhi.MD
   Formerly, professor and head of the department of
   Dermatology All India Institute of Medical sciences
   New Delhi , India

5. Reading this book by Dr. Ved Gossain brings to light the experience of many immigrants from all over the globe to the US. It defines struggles of a first generation caught between two different cultures. It involves giving up older traditions and assimilating new ones. This journey can be challenging but eventually may be rewarding. The text defines various stages of adaptation that an immigrant goes through to reach a stage of stability and relative assimilation and comfort. It is a tug of war between going back to one's native culture

or country versus adjusting to live in a newly adopted one. The book also takes us through personal tribulations and loss of Dr. Gossan's first wife. The text also compares, and contrasts arranged marriage by family arrangement vs. love marriage with cohabitation. It describes how these two different approaches to marriage have certain advantages and disadvantages. Moreover, the book describes how Dr. Gossain rose in the academic ladder to become Chief of Endocrinology and Associate Chair of Medicine at Michigan State University, all this speaking to his courage and skills. However, as many immigrants feel that they are not the prime choice for leadership positions, such as Department Chair. The world is not perfect, and the hope is always that the children of the first-generation immigrant will be better equipped to achieve what could have been due their parents. On a personal note, as an immigrant myself I can identify with much of Dr. Gossan's experience.

George S. Abela, MD

Professor of Medicine

Chief, division of Cardiology

Michigan State University

East Lansing Michigan. USA

6. Dr. V. V. Gossan's My Journey to the United States is a vivid autographical description of an Indian physician who emigrated to United States of America in the mid-1960s and steered his personal and professional life in the new land of opportunity during the next half a century. It is a beautiful commentary on the long process of acculturation which an immigrant and his family accept and adopt to settle in the new culture while firmly preserving their Indian roots at the same time.

Dr. Gossan's journey begins with understanding of local accent of language, system of medical care and perception of new environment. Completing the required clinical training, beginning with the new medical job, successfully climbing the professional ladder of academic achievements, and finally winning national and international accolades at home and abroad and at the same time raising the family with small kids proved to be an arduous task that any prospective immigrant must be acquainted with.

This autography is a story of diligence, courage, and resilience as well as despair, discrimination, and challenge of bereavement. Despair because of innumerable moments of anguish both at home in India and in the U.S., discrimination because of a self-perception of being a foreigner and above all, into just 10 years in the U.S., the bereavement on account of young Mrs. Gossan's demise at the age of 36 years due to leukemia leaving two children aged 5 and 6 behind for her husband to care for. This indeed turned the life of entire family topsy-turvy and compelled them to think of going back to India, a dilemma that they somehow tided over. There are so many positive ingredients like nostalgia, happiness and achievements and many not so positive ingredients like moments of sadness, emotional setbacks, and unpleasant sentiments in this autography that the story can be told in innumerable other ways like filmic autography and so on.

The dilemma of bringing up, educating, and settling the children in life was also somehow later solved as Dr. Gossain luckily soon found a highly worthy partner from a family well known to his family. They are now a happy family with three grown up kids well settled in life.

Length of this autography spanning over 160 pages is its real strength and there is much to be learned from repeated readings of this story.

Dr. Vinod Kumar.

Formerly,

Professor of Medicine, All India Institute of Medical Sciences. New Delhi,

Expert Advisory Member for Ageing & Health, World Health Organization

Recipient of Life Time Achievement Award in Ageing from Government of India.

7. Very interesting & engrossing story of an immigrant from India to USA. He came for adventure rather than to fulfill the American dream, about which he had no idea. Imagine a, highly qualified physician (doctorate in Medicine) landing at JFK with $8.00 in his pocket, not sure if it will be enough to convey him to his destination. But he did it, keeping his head high. He underwent a partial transformation of his personality, his culture and vocabulary , learning & interpreting conversations in a new way, quite often adding humor in daily life. Returned to India briefly, had an arranged marriage to a physician and started a new chapter of life feeling on the top of the world with 2 children & an inspiring wife. unfortunately, it did not last long when his lovely wife left for heavenly abode at age 36. He has very nicely described his disappointments & struggles in daily and professional life in a university setting but ultimately achieving his goals. I thoroughly enjoyed reading it and I highly recommend it.

Yash P. Kataria, MD

Professor Emeritus of Medicine : Director, Sarcoidosis Clinic:

Division of Pulmonary, Critical Care & Sleep Medicine

Brody School of Medicine

CONTENTS

Reviews i
Foreword viii
Preface x
Chapter 1: Introduction 1
Chapter 2: "Birth in Pakistan" 2
Chapter 3: Visiting Pakistan 6
Chapter 4: Early Childhood and admission to Medical school 10
Chapter 5: Getting a passport 20
Chapter 6: Coming To America 25
Chapter 7: The Journey Begins 28
Chapter 8: My First American Party 35
Chapter 9: My first visit to an American restaurant 37
Chapter 10: My first New Year Party 39
Chapter 11: Stage of Struggle 41
Chapter 12: Getting Married 51
Chapter 13: Fellowship and transition to Michigan State University 58
Chapter 14: Disaster Strikes 68
Chapter 15: Trip to India 89
Chapter 16: Getting Tenure 97
Chapter 17: The Acculturation Continues 112
Chapter 18: Preserving her memory 129
Chapter 19: Professional career 131
Chapter 20: Stage of Doubt 138
Chapter 21: Establishing Endocrinology Fellowship 146
Chapter 22: Awards 152
Chapter 23: Life Changing Event 155
Chapter 24: Stage of Giving 158
Chapter 25: Summary and Conclusions 166
References 175
Acknowledgments 179

FOREWORD

Dr. Ved Gossain and I were introduced in 1986, when I joined the Department of Medicine of the Michigan State University College of Human Medicine (MSUCHM) as a Health Services researcher. He was an astute, candid and gracious new colleague. What I did not know at the time was how his experience in coming to America from India created detours and round-abouts in the journey to becoming a specialist in Endocrinology. The importance of Ved's story is not just that he succeeded and thrived, it is how he shares his unique journey as an Indian immigrant. While he was poised to succeed anywhere, his training and career path led him through the extra twists and turns of a Foreign Medical Graduate, as we Americans labeled him

My late husband, Dr. David Rovner Professor of Medicine at the university of Michigan was already a highly regarded subspecialist with an international reputation. But he gave that up and moved to MSU CHM to help start a radical new medical school, the first community-integrated medical school, with a curriculum that emphasized a patient-centered philosophy and a biopsychosocial approach to caring for patients. The entire clinical education of medical students took place in community hospitals. When Dave recruited Ved to join the Department in 1975, he found a fellow adventurer, though as Ved's book reveals, not having a university hospital turned out to limit program development. David and Ved were kindred spirits. They were both highly sought-after clinicians and active research collaborators in a partnership that lasted for a quarter century. During this time, I also came to know Ved very well and this Foreword is from both of us.

Ved's book invites us to follow him on his journey through the extra hoops to obtain an American medical license, then on to his success as an accomplished clinician, researcher and administrator. He also describes the challenges of marriage, family life and family left behind in that not-quite-American status we often afford immigrant physicians even as they contribute to our health and well-being. Ved's reflections on his professional and personal journey illustrate how the extra dimension of going through the stages of acculturation shape the parallel experience of the journey from novice to expert physician.

During the time that he was in the USA, he did not forget his roots. He kept in contact with colleagues in India and gave back to his mother land as much as he could. In the 1990s, Ved invited David to join him on a three-week trip to teach continuing medical education courses in endocrinology, in India. While I would not be participating in the courses, I also went along. The trip gave me a taste of several things that figure prominently in the book. One was how it feels to be a foreigner. (In my tennis shoes and London Fog raincoat I was particularly noticeable). Another was the gracious manner of our hosts as they folded us into their activities and showed us the wonders of the cities of Mumbai, Chandīgarh and Hyderabad. And then, his children's bi-cultural upbringing showed when Ved's youngest son, about eight years old at the time, insisted we go to McDonald's for lunch in Delhi.

My husband David died in May 2020. In the last months before David's death, he enjoyed reading Ved's manuscript. It allowed him to revisit his and Ved's years of developing friendship, relying on each other as trusted colleagues to share the responsibilities and vagaries of academic medicine. As David said to me at that time, "the best thing I did in my MSU career was to hire Ved Gossain."

Margaret Holmes - Rovner, Ph.D
Prof. Emerita, Health Services Research.
David R. Rovner, MD, FACP
Professor Emeritus, Endocrinology and Metabolism

PREFACE

America is a land of immigrants. Every year thousands of immigrants come to the US, looking to fulfill their American dream. However, not every immigrant comes looking for the American dream. For those who have an American dream, some get to achieve their dream, and some do not. Regardless of whether the dream is fulfilled or not, every immigrant has a unique story to tell, and mine is not an exception. I arrived in this country as an adventure and to get advanced training in Endocrinology. I did not even know what the American dream was. I had intended to stay in this country for a maximum of three to five years, yet more than 50 years have passed, and I am still here. Coming from India, an entirely different culture and having spent the major part of my life in the US, I believe I have a story to tell, that I hope will be interesting, if not for anyone else then for my children, and possibly grand children who are so unfamiliar with the life and the culture of India. A part of my dream that has been fulfilled, i.e. becoming a professor of medicine, although I never even dreamt that it would be in the USA. My life, both from a professional and a personal standpoint, has had its ups and downs, the major one of which was the death of my spouse early in my career. She was an inspiration and remained so even in her death. The emotional roller coaster that I went through while she was ill and subsequently passed is vividly engraved in my memory. I can close my eyes and still feel those moments. I am therefore dedicating this book to her memory.

1
INTRODUCTION

I arrived in this country after having completed, not only my basic medical education (MB,BS which stands for Bachelor of Medicine and Bachelor of Surgery) but also having completed a residency in Internal Medicine. It required clinical training and a thesis to obtain an advanced degree in Medicine (M.D., Doctorate in Medicine). Thus, I was a "board certified" physician by Indian standards, but all that training was not recognized in the USA. Nevertheless, I had a solid foundation of medicine (Internal Medicine to be more specific) and I was able to recognize the basic differences of medical education and medical practice in India versus United States. I have attempted to describe some of those differences. My main objective for coming to the USA was to obtain additional training in Endocrinology (Endocrinology Fellowship),which was not available in India at that time and to return to India after that was completed. Over the years, through additional training I did become a "board certified" Endocrinologist, but for that I had to repeat three years of Internal Medicine residency that I didn't think that I needed and three additional years of training in Endocrinology. I have been fortunate to practice that specialty for more than 40 years and I have described some of the experiences I have had, which remain vivid memories even after so many years.

2
"BIRTH IN PAKISTAN"

I was the youngest of 9 children, born in a small village in undivided India. The village is now in Pakistan. I was born at home, brought into this world with the help of either my grandmother or the local midwife. There is no "official" record of my birth. Therefore, I am not even certain about the exact date of my birth. My "official" birthday was recorded on the first day of my schooling, that is, the day my father decided that I was 5 years old and ready to begin school. My father was a teacher and the only graduate (B.A.) in our large extended family and believed in early education. Consequently, I am quite sure that I must have been about four or 4 ½ years old, and he convinced the school authorities that I was 5 years old and should begin schooling. No "official" birth certificates were required as the proof of age at that time. The date recorded at the time of admission became my "official" date of birth. It finally was also included in the high school diploma that I received at the time of graduation from high school. That is the only proof of my date of birth that I have. That date of birth has been accepted as the "true" date of birth for all official purposes in India and abroad.

I remember our old house with a large compound in the middle, where we all (grandparents, uncles, aunts and several cousins) lived as one large extended family. The family was close knit, to the extent that cousins were not referred to as cousins, but we were all simply brothers and sisters. It would seem that to manage a family of 9 children would be a difficult, if not impossible, task for any mother. However, in this setting it was not a problem at all. There were several aunts in the household who were there to help. Moreover at least three of my five older sisters were like second mothers to me. My memories are that it was fun growing up with cousins. We did not have to go out of the house to look for friends to play with.

In any event, the time of my birth was not particularly an opportune time to be born in that part of the world. The seed for dividing India and creating "Pakistan" had already been planted, and it was all but inevitable that Pakistan would be created, the only question was when and how. The resolution to create Pakistan was adopted by the Muslim League (the political party responsible for creation of Pakistan) on March 23, 1940. That spot is now marked by a 60-meter-high tower, known as Minar-e-Pakistan, and to this day, March 23rd is celebrated as "Pakistan Day" in Pakistan (1). Pakistan was finally created on August 14, 1947. The Independence Day for Pakistan is August 14, whereas for India it is August 15. Although it was not planned or anticipated, it led to hundreds of thousands of Muslims migrating to Pakistan from India and hundreds of thousands of Hindus and Sikhs migrating from the newly created Pakistan to now the divided India. It also led to one of the largest civil wars in our history.

Over a million people died in the violence and nearly 14 and a half million people moved both ways across the newly created borders. Muslims were murdering innocent Hindus, and in turn, Hindus were killing innocent Muslims. Atrocities and crimes against humanity of untold proportion were committed.

While the atrocities received worldwide attention, there were also a few heart-warming stories, where many Muslims in Pakistan and many Hindus in India went out of their way, even at great personal risk to their own lives to help people of the opposite religion. These people had lived together for years in the undivided India and were best of friends, but the politics had changed the whole landscape and these people were being forced to move. Many Muslims hid their Hindu friends to save them from Muslims who were bent upon killing those Hindus and vice versa. One such story in our own family is where a friend of my brother-in-law (Sister's husband), asked his father, who was a police commissioner in the newly created Pakistan to escort the family of my brother-in-law across the border to safety in India. They were escorted to the border, said their goodbyes, and promised to remain in touch if possible. Just as they were about to part, the Pakistani friend realized that his departing friend had no cash on him. They both returned to the house that my brother-in-law had just abandoned for good, broke open a trunk (a large suitcase made of steel) in which the cash was stashed and obtained some cash. The Pakistani friend, then, had a bunch of cash buried and sealed in the sole of my brother-in-law's shoes, to avoid being detected and yet making sure that they would have some money once they crossed the border into India.

Although I was too young to remember all the details, I do remember the dusk to dawn curfews and Muslims shouting "Allah-hu-Akbar" (God is great) and Hindus shouting "Har-Har-Mahadev" (Hindu God is great). Our immediate nuclear family escaped all the atrocities because we had left our home in Pakistan for summer vacation (In July 1947) to join my brother, who was employed in India. Shortly after that, my uncles, aunts, and several cousins arrived as well. They told stories about, how they had witnessed murders at the border, how women were abducted and raped repeatedly and how some Hindu men had killed their own daughters and other women folks to prevent them from being attacked or worse, raped by Muslims. I do remember about 30 or 40 relatives living in a 2-bedroom house: all the women sleeping in one room on the floor, and all the men in another room. Being a small child, I remember sleeping on the only dining table in the house. While this was comfortable, I remember being afraid that I might fall during the night and break my head or break a bone.

The only earning member of the family at that time was my brother, and although we never went without food, I still remember the sinking sensation at the time of breakfast or lunch, whether there would be enough food for everyone at dinner time.

Gradually, however, the process of rehabilitation of the family began. My father was a teacher. He found a job in a local school. My uncles, who were in business, found places to re-establish their business in another town, and thus, out of necessity, the one large happy extended family got broken up into several small units. Although our family was not alone in this process, it was painful. Not only had the country been divided, but it also felt like our family had been divided, and although these various family units remained close, it was nowhere as close as it used to be while living in the same old house.

3

VISITING PAKISTAN

I was able to visit Pakistan in the year 2006. I have had a very strong desire to go to Pakistan (The place of my birth) but due to the relations between India and Pakistan, it was not possible until I had acquired US citizenship. Even after that, I was apprehensive of going there because of the history of adverse relations between Hindus and Muslims. It finally happened in the year 2006 when a young physician who had completed his Nephrology (diseases of the Kidney) training at the University of Cincinnati and now a very prominent Nephrologist in Lahore, invited a classmate of mine, who had been his program director at the University of Cincinnati to visit him in Lahore. My classmate had known about my desire to visit Pakistan, so he invited me to go along. I was so happy and jumped at the opportunity. The visit to Pakistan was one of the most wonderful trips I had taken in my lifetime. We crossed the border at Amritsar (Wagah border) on foot. This is a unique border, probably the only one of its kind in the world, where every evening there is a parade of Pakistani and Indian border security forces, both sides presenting their best. The audience on both sides shouts patriotic slogans, like "Pakistan Zindabad" (long live Pakistan) and "Jai Bharat Mata Ki" (Long live mother India). It is a parade worth watching if one gets an opportunity to do so.

Before we entered Pakistan, there was a passport control station. The officer on duty, spoke the same language that we all did (Punjabi).

He was a very jovial fellow and related several jokes and a few "sheyrs", a type of Urdu poetry. In the process, although he completed all the formalities that he needed to, he made the experience very entertaining.

We were received by our host as we entered Pakistan. He had not only brought with him a large sum of Pakistani currency, so we would not get cheated by some unscrupulous characters at the border, but also had brought packed lunch for all of us. (Altogether we were four couples).Contrary to what might be perceived in the political world, the people on the street were very friendly and welcoming, particularly to our Sikh friends who were readily recognized as visitors due to their head gear (Turbans).

We met a gentleman, who was a friend of our host. In just about a few minutes after the introductions were completed, he said, "All of you are having dinner with me tonight". We were impressed by his genuine desire to do so, and we accepted his invitation. As a result, we all went to the "Food Street" in Lahore. It is a street full of vendors who were selling different kinds of foods. You could find a seat in the restaurant of any of the vendors and order food from any of the shops on that street and they brought whatever food you had ordered. It was a delicious experience. At the end, our host paid the bill at the restaurant where we were seated. How they finally divided the amount among themselves is beyond me.

The next day, we travelled to the village where I was born. Once again, due to the apprehensions mentioned above, I asked our host if he could send someone local to accompany us on this trip. He easily arranged for a midlevel administrator from his hospital to accompany us. On our way, we stopped in Lyallpur (Now called Faisalabad). One of my aunts who had lived there for several years, had given me a brief description of downtown. There was a central tower and six streets that radiated from it. Each street had a unique market, such as clothing, jewelry etc. It was interesting to see that her description was still accurate, but perhaps it also speaks for the fact that even after almost 60 years not much had changed in that part of the city. We then moved on towards my village (Jhang Maghiana). My older brother had drawn me a map. I was somewhat pleasantly surprised that the map was still accurate. Without much difficulty, I was able to locate the street on which we had lived (Incidentally, it was called Gossain street before partition, now called something else). It was (is) located next to the Bank street, which is still known by the same name. I was able to locate our old house. (See picture)

Gossain Street as seen in 2006

*Elementary school attended
With Ramma in 2006*

Unfortunately, the house was locked, but I was able to peep through the main door and was able to identify the general appearance of the house. A local person joined us, uninvited and acted as the guide. He then was able to take me to the elementary school where I had studied.

In those days it was officially called "King George Primary school", but the locals knew it as the Talab walla school (The school with a pond). The pond had now dried, and the school was now known as "Sadhu Ram Muslim High School," (Interestingly, Sadhu Ram is a Hindu name, but the word Muslim has been added to the full name of the school). I was also able to locate the high school where my older brothers had studied, and my father had taught. Adjacent to the high schools was the college where my brothers had studied. At that time, it was only a 2-year college but now they were awarding bachelor's and master's degrees. As we were walking around the campus, the Principal of the college, who lived on campus saw us and invited us to his house. He welcomed us with open arms, and we had a nice conversation. It was a very pleasant experience. I felt as if I was meeting an old friend after a long time. In addition, I was also able to locate the girl's school where my sisters had studied.

On our way back to Lahore, it got dark, and it was time for the driver to say his evening prayers (Namaaz). He asked if he could stop at the mosque and pray to which we readily agreed. After his prayers, he asked if he could take a small diversion to visit with his father, who was old and now lived alone.

Before he did that, he also went ahead and relayed to us that just a few days before on that very street a taxi had been robbed and the passengers murdered. As a result of that, while he visited his father and we waited in the taxi outside, both my wife and I spent a few anxious moments. He returned in a few minutes and we proceeded on our way back to Lahore. Despite all this, altogether, it was a wonderful nostalgic trip and I have very fond memories of that visit, which I will carry with me for a long time to come. I should also add that I came away with the impression that an average person on the street would very much like to be friendly with its neighboring nation (India), but the political realities are quite different.

4

EARLY CHILDHOOD AND ADMISSION TO MEDICAL SCHOOL

The remainder of my childhood was pretty uneventful. I completed high school and 3 years of college successfully. Getting into pre-medical program was also not difficult. At that time, most boys entered either into engineering or medicine as a profession (and women went into teaching). Our family was (is) full of engineers, so just to do something different, I opted for medicine. Getting admission to a medical school was also not a problem since the admission was based almost exclusively on the grades obtained in pre-med courses and my grades were high enough to assure admission. There was, however, a small hitch and that was, a requirement that the applicants be the resident of the state where they were applying for admission to the medical school, namely Punjab in my case. After the partition of the country, I had grown up in a different state (Uttar Pradesh). To attend the Medical college in Amritsar, it was required that we establish that I was a resident of Punjab. That would be possible, but not easy. After partition of the country, we had been given land in Punjab, to compensate for the property that we had lost in Pakistan. Such compensations were mutually agreed upon by the two governments (India and Pakistan). Land ownership would thus establish our residency in Punjab, but it would require a certificate from the district magistrate of the district where we owned the land.

This would not be an easy task because of the government bureaucracy and would probably have required bribing the officers concerned. However, as luck would have it, the district magistrate of the district (Rohtak) turned out to be the brother-in-law of a close friend of my brother. When we mentioned this in a casual conversation to him, he simply stated that a letter documenting our residency status would arrive at our house in a few days, and that is exactly what happened. Thus, a task that would have required myself and my father going to Rohtak and spending several days and probably bribing someone was simplified in one stroke of luck. Events like this have restored my faith in the theory that destiny is predetermined.

I was admitted to Medical College Amritsar after a brief, very informal interview, following which I not only felt relieved but proud since the Medical College Amritsar in those days was ranked as one of the top 3 or top 5 medical schools in the country. There are probably more than 500 medical schools in India now and ranking them would be a difficult, if not an impossible task.

Although getting admission to the medical school was not a problem, the financial aspect of that was a problem and could have derailed the trajectory of my career and thus my life. It may seem strange to the medical students in this country (USA) who incur a great deal of debt before they graduate from medical school, that paying for the medical school in India was (and still is) the responsibility of the parents, rather than the students themselves. This may be partly because at the time of the entry to the medical school the students in India are barely 17 years old. In addition, no student loans were available in those days. Even today, although the loans are available, they are hard to come by in India. In my case, it was even more of a problem because by this time my father had retired and he was not able to provide for my medical education, even though all his life he had emphasized the importance of education. Consequently, the financial burden of my medical education fell upon the shoulders of my three older brothers. I will never know the details, but collectively they decided to support our family and my medical education for which I will remain indebted to them forever.

The medical curriculum started with introduction to the "dissection hall" where we were assigned bodies for dissection to study anatomy. We completed the dissection of the entire human body and when we finished, we knew every little nerve, artery and bone that existed in the human body. Every week we used to have a test on the anatomy of the parts that we had dissected. The test was in the form of an oral test and the instructors made sure that everyone failed at least once. It was their way of making sure that we learned the material as well as possible. It also put the fear in everyone's mind that medical school studies were difficult and would require everyone's best effort to succeed. I must admit that this strategy worked. The study of anatomy over the years has been much simplified and made much easier for medical students. Many medical schools in the USA do not require the dissection of the human body but they are assigned to a cadaver that has been dissected by someone else and they can learn the things that they need to learn from this body. At the end of two years of studying Anatomy and Physiology there was the "First Professional Examination", which consisted of theory and practical exams (labs). The theory questions were of the essay type and included the entire two-year curriculum. We were given the choice of answering 5 questions out of the 6 included in the examination paper, to be completed over a three-hour time. The questions could be "trace the course of the Femoral artery from its origin to the ankle". One was expected to describe that including the major branches on its way. Or "describe the consequences of the injury to the brachial plexus and include the names of the muscles affected". In physiology, similar essay type questions may be "describe the process of erythropoiesis" (Development of the red blood cells) or "describe the process of bone remodeling". As is evident, these types of questions are much more difficult to answer than the typical multiple-choice questions. To make matters worse, if you did not know the subject of the question being asked, the consequences could be dire. It was also an important milestone. One had only two attempts to pass this exam, and if not successful, you were required to repeat the courses of the previous year. One got two more attempts (total of 4) to pass the "First Professional Examination", and if still not successful, one was asked to leave the medical school and look for another career. Needless to add that it was a very stressful time for all of us. Every year about 5 to 10 % of the class would leave the medical school because of inability to pass the "First Professional Exam" in four attempts.

The clinical years were more challenging and interesting. Many of the diseases we saw in those days are not prevalent anymore and certainly are not commonly seen in this part of the world (USA). Rheumatic heart disease with its consequent damage to the heart valves was fairly common. Each valvular lesion results in typical change in the heart sounds and produces additional sounds called murmurs. It was a challenge to identify the characteristic murmurs and thereby make an accurate diagnosis of the underlying defect of the particular valve. Similarly, the changes in the breath sounds resulting from different diseases like tuberculosis are typical and were a challenge to identify. We were expected to identify the underlying lesion like fluid in the pleural cavity and then identify the cause of these changes. (Pleura is a two layered membrane that surrounds the lungs. The space between the two layers is the pleural cavity). In this case the cause may be tuberculosis, cancer, or a simple pneumonia. The emphasis on the clinical diagnostic skills was enormous and we were tested on these skills before graduating. Even in our lectures, once the professors had described all the modern ways to diagnose and treat an illness, they would say, "OK, if you are now in a remote village and encounter such a patient, what would you do", again emphasizing the clinical skills needed to manage patients with very limited facilities. Typically, for the final exam we were given a "long case" and a "short case". In the long case we were expected to obtain a thorough history, do a complete physical exam, and come up with a clinical diagnosis. This was followed by the examiner' s questions about the diagnostic and therapeutic plans that would be needed for the management of the patient under discussion.

In the short cases, the students were asked to examine a particular area of the body, such as the heart. Based entirely on the clinical exam, without even talking to the patient, we were expected to come up with a clinical diagnosis and be able to defend it. There was a lot less emphasis on laboratory tests and radiological testing, mainly because these modalities were expensive and not readily available.

I can recall instituting treatment for tuberculosis based on the clinical exam without even having a chest X-ray or sputum testing. These tests would be ordered but might not be available for a few days or a few weeks in some instances and it was considered inadvisable to delay the treatment. When the laboratory results and the X-rays became available in a few days or a few weeks, the diagnosis could be revised if needed.

This education was in marked contrast to what I would observe in the US. Even today, the USMLE (US Medical License Examination) part I, II and III are entirely based on multiple choice type questions. The clinical exam simply is a test of the student's ability to be able to obtain a history and perform a brief physical examination. The scoring is set at a level, such that 95% of the US senior Medical students pass these exams on their first attempt. There appears to be a lot less emphasis on the clinical diagnosis and much more reliability on the lab tests and other diagnostic modalities such as X-rays and CT scans. I can distinctly recall that back in 1967, a medical student from Yale, while I was a resident at the Springfield Hospital Medical Center (now Bay State Medical Center) in Springfield, Massachusetts, had examined a patient with Rheumatoid arthritis. I asked him what are the changes that we might expect in the lungs of such a patient and what physical findings did he notice in the patient under discussion. He responded that he had not examined the lungs of the patient. When asked why? His response was "because we are going to get a chest X-ray anyway." I was somewhat taken aback by his response. Admittedly, the chest X-ray is much more sensitive than the clinical exam but that does not mean that we can ignore or skip the clinical exam altogether. Over the years, as the cost of medicine, especially in the US has increased, several professional organizations are now advocating to "choose wisely", meaning to rely more on the clinical exams and order only those lab tests that are absolutely essential.

The medical school curriculum was as rigorous as anywhere else. It was greatly influenced by the medical education in UK. I graduated on time, without any "hiccups" along the way.

During the year of internship, the thoughts of going abroad to study further began to crop up in my mind. At that time, the higher education in medicine was thought to be best in UK but USA was fast catching up. Although a degree from Medical College Amritsar would be treated as at par with any medical degree obtained in UK, as per the rules of the General Medical council of UK at that time, the US did not recognize any medical degrees from abroad except for Canada. In 1956 a private nonprofit organization, the Evaluation Service for Foreign Medical Graduates was established to provide information and answer inquiries of IMGs (International Medical graduates, previously also called Foreign Medical Graduates), planning to come to United States for Graduate Medical Education (GME). It also evaluated IMGs credentials, knowledge of Medicine and command of English language and certify that IMGs have met certain medical education requirements and were considered "competent" to enter a US residency program. Later, it was renamed as ECFMG (Educational Commission for Foreign Medical Graduates). The ECFMG validated (and still does) the medical credentials of foreign medical graduates (FMGs) and conducted a standardized exam to ascertain the readiness of FMGs to train in the US hospitals. Consequently, in the years 1963/64, to find a position in the USA, one would have to pass the test administered by the ECFMG. The ECFMG used to publish a guidebook to familiarize foreign graduates with the multiple-choice type questions and the example they used was:

Heart belongs to which system?

- Gastrointestinal
- Pulmonary
- Cardiovascular
- Neurological

Obviously, an easy question.

So, one day while biking from our hostel (dorm) to the hospital (that was our mode of transportation from the medical school to our dormitories to the hospital and back) a fellow intern said "Ved! Let us take that American exam". I said, "What is that"? He went on to explain the ECFMG exam and said it is really very easy because the type of questions they ask are like "Heart belongs to which system?"

In any event we decided to apply to take the exam.

The application required photocopies of one's diploma and some other documents. In those days, there was no place in Amritsar where one could obtain photocopies. So, we went to a photographer and had the original diplomas photographed. Anecdotally, I might add that those photocopies were accepted as if they were originals. Contrary to that, in today's environment, photocopies are not accepted, and the original transcripts are forwarded to hospitals, ECFMG or licensing agencies directly from the medical schools, presumably to avoid any fraud. Has fraud in medical profession increased so much that we must resort to this? I recall that in my later years here in the USA, I was recruiting a physician to be on our faculty. We obtained the usual references where he had worked in the last few years. He had been employed by the US Navy many years ago. The University administration required me to obtain references from the Navy, even though he had documents showing that he was honorably discharged. I wonder that if I was to request original transcripts from my medical school, would they be available today? The application also required an application fee of $50.00. However, in those days, the Reserve Bank of India would not allow any foreign exchange for this purpose. Therefore, almost every applicant included a statement with their application that the fee could not be paid at the time of application.

The ECFMG, perhaps under instructions from the State department, almost always waived this fee to encourage doctors to take the exam and ultimately come to the USA. ECFMG would write to the applicants to obtain a statement from the Reserve Bank of India to support the fact that the foreign exchange was not available. This statement was not difficult to obtain for those who received such a letter from the ECFMG. Although many of my colleagues got such a letter, I never received one. I still remember the last date for the receipt of the application was January 6th, and I had mailed my application on Dec 30th. Naturally, I assumed that my application was not received by ECFMG by the deadline and hence I had not heard from them. Since going to the USA was not a high priority at that time, I did not care about that.

The time passed and suddenly one day in March/April 1964 I saw several of my friends packing up to go to New Delhi to take the ECFMG exam. I must admit that I felt a little envious or even jealous that all these guys will take the exam, and they will be able to go to USA if they so choose, but I would not. As I was contemplating these thoughts, a colleague ran into me and said "Ved! Are you not going to New Delhi?" I said, "No, perhaps my application never made it in time, so I am not able to take the test". He said, "But I saw your admission ticket for the exam in the mail room. You better hurry up and check the mail room."

It was 4 o'clock in the afternoon, and the mail room closed at 5 PM. So, I ran to the mail room and asked the mailroom clerk if there was a letter for me from America. He replied, "I have not seen any, but sometimes the letters get mixed up. If you want to look, go ahead." I asked him what time he would close the mail room? He replied "do not worry, look all you want and I will wait for you". I felt relieved and began looking and guess what, sure enough the admission ticket was there. However, it was mixed up with the letters intended for the patients in the orthopedic ward.

I have been a strong believer, that our destiny is predetermined. If this was not destiny, I do not know what is, because after finding that letter I was on my way to New Delhi on the train that departed at 9 PM. On the train, I noted, some of my colleagues with their medical books cramming up for the exam. I must admit, that I also thought that I also should be studying for the exam. However, considering the fact that I had not studied for it any way, I decided it was best to depend on what I had learned in the previous several years rather than try to catch up while traveling in the train. Consequently, I decided to take it easy and went to sleep, as much as it was possible to sleep in the crowded Indian trains, which incidentally have become even more crowded in the recent years.

Next morning, I arrived at my sister's place unannounced, and she was surprised. I explained to her and her husband the purpose of my visit and requested my brother-in-law to drop me off at the "Vigyan Bhawan", the site of the examination.

When we arrived there, we were surprised to see so many young doctors who had also arrived to take the exam. My brother-in-law could not help himself and asked, "Are all these doctors going to America?" I replied that this was only the first step in the process, for those who want to go.

The exam itself was difficult and challenging, mostly because of its format of multiple-choice questions, which most of the test takers, including myself were not very familiar with. The exam also included a test of spoken English language. For that test, an American instructor related the story "Mary had a little lamb." We were required to answer questions like "Who had a little lamb?", and "What did Mary have?" etc. The idea was to see if we understood English language spoken in the American accent.

A few weeks later the test results arrived in mail. Fortunately, I passed the exam at the level of the minimal score required to pass (75). These days the old ECFMG exam has been replaced by United States Medical license exam (USMLE) I and II. This allows the FMGs to establish that their training and credentials are equal to those of the US medical graduates (USMGS). Although I was glad to have passed the exam but kept the result in a drawer since I had no plans to go to America at that time.

Anecdotally, I might add that the ECFMG exam, which was only a day long was later replaced by Visa qualifying exam and now has been replaced by USMLE I, USMLEII, Clinical Knowledge (CK) and clinical skills exam (CS) before the students become eligible to apply for a residency position in the USA. Needless to say, that these exams are more extensive than the previously administered ECFMG exam, but they may not necessarily be more discriminatory. However, for those who pass these exams, it certifies for all IMGS, no matter where they went to medical school that their medical and clinical knowledge is as good as US graduating medical students.

5
GETTING A PASSPORT

As a first step for going abroad to study in the UK or USA, an application for obtaining a passport was made. However, for almost a year, there was no response from the passport office of government of India. Later on, we found out through a grapevine that the government of India had decided not to issue passports to physicians to prevent the brain drain of physicians.

Meanwhile, my internship (house job) was finished, going abroad did not appear to be a viable option, and one had to decide the next course of action. I was fortunate to be able to obtain the position of an assistant research officer under a scheme (Research Project) of the Indian council of medical research (ICMR). The principal investigator for the research project was professor, MMS Ahuja (Now deceased) at the All-India Institute of Medical Sciences (AIIMS) and the appointment of research officers was entirely at his discretion. A few months later, I was also selected as one of the residents in General Medicine (Internal Medicine). AIIMS was and continues to be one of the premium medical institutions in India. It has been called the "NIH" of India. Thus, this position would provide an opportunity to complete the residency as well as to obtain an advanced, postdoctoral degree in medicine (M.D.). It would also require carrying on a research project, submitting and defending a thesis. For the research, the simultaneous appointment as a research officer for the Indian council of Medical research, would not only provide an opportunity to conduct research but it will also provide the funds needed to conduct the research. The funds also provided me a salary, about 550 rupees a month. This was a good amount of money in those days and was also much more than what the post graduate students (Residents) were receiving as their stipend (200 Rupees a month). Thus, it provided the highly desirable combination of more money, funds for the research and simultaneously pursuing the residency in Internal Medicine and obtain the degree of MD (Doctorate in Medicine). I was fortunate to have become a mentee of late Professor MMS Ahuja and began to work on a thesis entitled "Dietetic analysis, blood lipids, chemical and isotopic studies in Indian diabetics and their relation to vascular complications", which eventually was published in the American journal of Clinical Nutrition. It was also my first introduction to the discipline of Endocrinology which eventually became my career. I might also add that over the ensuing years the department of Endocrinology at AIIMS became a very fertile ground for training Endocrinologists and a large number of Endocrinologists practicing in India and some even abroad were trained in that unit.

It was during these residency years, I discovered that one of my colleagues had filed a lawsuit in Bombay High court against the Indian government for blocking the issuance of passports to physicians and he had won the lawsuit. Although it was disappointing that I had not received the passport when it was applied for, it was reassuring that law and order, the rights of citizens and the democratic process, was functioning well in India. Perhaps as a result of that lawsuit, one day suddenly, the passport arrived in the mail, again stimulating the desire to go abroad. However, by this time, I was almost halfway through the residency program and the MD degree, and it made no sense to abandon that program halfway. The residency was completed in May 1967. A few weeks before that, I had secured a job (as a medical officer) in a factory managed by Municipal Corporation of Delhi. I informed the employer that I would start the job, only after completion of the residency. When I started that job, it became clear that it was an unsatisfying job in terms of the skills needed, but it provided money to put food on the table. The patient population was almost entirely the labor force that worked at the factory. I would attend to the minor injuries, common colds and fill out forms for them to obtain medical leave from work. One of the benefits for employees was the drug coverage but that was available only if the prescription was written by one of the factory doctors. So patients would go to AIIMS, get a prescription written and would ask me to re write that prescription, so that they could get it for free. In addition, I found out that some of them would go to the drug store and instead of actually getting the prescription filled, they would trade it for cosmetics for their wives or whatever. Going abroad suddenly began to look attractive again. Meanwhile, there were open positions at AIIMS as Registrars (lecturers) in Medicine. As a recent graduate from the residency at AIIMS, this job was mine for asking, and I was all set to apply for the job (and had been assured by the Professor (Professor Ahuja) who was also the head of the Endocrine Department, that the job was mine if I wanted it). At that point in my career, this would have been the most coveted position I could ask for. Naturally, I was very happy at the thoughts of having a highly satisfying academic career at one of the most prestigious (if not the most prestigious) medical institutions of the country. However, destiny had something else in mind. A casual conversation with a senior colleague, who had just finished his registrar ship, changed the course of my life. It went something like this:

Dr. Upadhyay: Dr. Gossain, what are you doing these days?
Me: "I am working for Municipal Corporation of Delhi, but I am thinking of changing jobs."
Dr. Upadhyay: "So, if you give up that job, what will you do?"
Me: "I can get a job at AIIMS as a registrar. Prof. Ahuja says that the job is mine; all I have to do is to apply or I have a position in America in one of the hospitals."
Dr. Upadhyay: "So, if you become a registrar, what will you be doing after 3 years." (Registrar positions like the residencies were time limited for 3 years.)

Me:	"Hopefully, I will get a position as an Assistant Professor in the Endocrinology Department, and I will be on my way towards an academic career."
Dr. Upadhyay:	"That is always possible, and I wish you luck. However, whatever you do, can you help me get the job that you will relinquish?"
Me:	(Laughingly) "Don't be joking with me. You should be getting a position as an Assistant Professor (just like I had hoped) either here itself or at some other medical school in the country."
Dr. Upadhyay:	"Yes! That is true and actually I was hoping for that too. However, the fact of the matter is that As of July 1 (1967), I don't have a job, and I have a wife and two kids to feed."

He then went on to say "Take my advice, go to America, do an Endocrinology Fellowship (In those days, there were no recognized Endocrinology Fellowships in India.) And when you return, you should have no trouble finding a position as an Assistant Professor anywhere in India." It made a lot of sense, and I decided at that point, to change the course of action. I was now going to USA for an Endocrinology Fellowship and return to India after becoming 'board certified" in Endocrinology. My estimate was that it would take 3 to 5 years to achieve that goal.

That evening, when I went back to my apartment, I pulled out the letter that I had received from Springfield Hospital, Springfield, Mass., to which I had paid no attention for the last few weeks. I noticed that they had offered me a position as an intern. Having recently graduated with the MD degree from AIIMS, I felt it was beneath my dignity to go to that hospital and work as an intern, and I fired a letter back to the hospital stating exactly that. Within a few days, I got a nice response back stating that they had offered me that position because if I ever wanted to get a license to practice medicine in Massachusetts, a year of internship was required. If I did not care for that, I could come to the hospital as a 2nd year resident. I gladly accepted that job. At that time, I had no intention of settling in the USA. I began preparing to leave.

(By this time also the glory of higher medical education in the UK had faded and clearly the medical education in the USA was at the top.)

It was my intention to stay in the USA only for as long as it took to complete an Endocrinology fellowship and return to India. As described below, it obviously did not happen.

6

COMING TO AMERICA

It was already the beginning of the month of July, and by the time I would get a visa to go to USA and complete other formalities, clearly the month of July would be over. So, I sent a letter to the hospital that I would start the job on August 1 even though the hospital wanted me to start on July 1st. They accepted this arrangement. A few days before my departure, I informed the hospital by mail that I would be arriving on July 31 (There were no cell phones in those days, and it was difficult to connect with overseas calls and they were expensive). The letter actually arrived after I had reached Springfield, Mass. (It is relevant later.)

With all the formalities completed including obtaining a Visa (J1 category) I boarded a flight from New Delhi for Bradly Field (airport for Springfield Mass and Hartford Connecticut) on July 26, 1967, spent a couple of days in London with a friend from medical school and arrived in New York on July 31. Imagine reaching the JFK airport in New York with $8.00 in your pocket. That was the amount that the government of India allowed in those days in the form of foreign exchange, and that was all the money I had in my possession. I took a connecting flight from JFK to Bradley Field (Springfield/Hartford) airport which was already paid for. From there, I had to take a bus to downtown Springfield; the bus fare being $5.00. On reaching Bradley

Field or at least after reaching downtown Springfield, I was expecting someone from the hospital to come and pick me up, but no such luck. In those days, because of the doctor shortage it was customary for the hospitals to send someone from the administration to receive the incoming doctors. Not only that, but many hospitals also paid for the doctor's airfare, or extended a loan to the doctors for their air ticket. Since there was no one from the hospital to receive me, the only alternative, for me was to take a cab to reach the hospital. But with only $3.00 in my pocket, it did not seem like an easy task. Nevertheless, I gingerly approached a cab and asked the driver if he could take me to Springfield hospital. With a smile, he said "Hop right in."

Me: "Before I get in, I need to know what the fare would be."
Cab Driver: "About two dollars."
Me: "Are you sure, no more than $2.00?"
Cab Drive: "Maybe $2.50 at the most."
Me: "Are you sure! No more than $2.50?"
Cab Driver: "Oh yes! Definitely, no more than $2.50." (That was 1967, Now a days it costs more than that, just to get into a cab). I felt a sense of relief and hopped in the cab.

On reaching the hospital, I approached the reception desk, introduced myself, and stated that I was one of the new residents.

Hospital Receptionist: "I have no information that you are a resident and that you will be arriving today."
Me: (Somewhat sheepishly) "Well! I am here. Do you want to see the letter that the hospital sent me?"
Hospital Receptionist: "No, but where are you from?"
Me: "India."
Hospital Receptionist: "Ok, give me a few minutes and let me see what I can do for you."

She made a few calls and a few minutes later one Dr. Iyengar, a 5th year surgical resident, who also happened to be from India, came to pick me up. He escorted me to the cafeteria and said, "Help yourself to any food items that you want. Food for residents is free." It was about 5 pm and according to my thinking it was "teatime", not realizing that it was dinner time, and that the cafeteria would close by 6:30 pm. I, therefore, picked up a muffin and a cup of tea. Dr. Iyengar, somewhat surprisingly said "That is all you're going to have?" but he forgot to mention that the cafeteria would close by 6:30 pm. After that brief encounter in the cafeteria, Dr. Iyengar, literally handed me over to the Chief Resident in Medicine, one Dr. Gurpal Singh Kingra, who also happened to be from India. I was surprised (pleasantly of course) that the first couple of residents that I had met were fellow Indians.

Around 9 pm, he (Dr. Kingra) asked me if I was hungry. When I replied in the affirmative, he went on to say, "I am sorry, but I have nothing to feed you, and I don't even have a car to take you out to a restaurant. If you are very hungry, I can take you to the hospital and we can get a few slices of bread." We finally decided that it was not worth going to the hospital, and I was not going to starve to death.

A few minutes later, he asked "Where are you going to sleep tonight?" Of course, I had no idea. Although the hospital was also going to provide accommodation, no room was assigned to me (at least not to our knowledge) and hence none was available; most likely because the hospital had not yet received the letter informing them of my arrival. He finally came upon the idea that we could climb through a window and use one of the unoccupied rooms which were assigned to the house staff. To make matters worse, my luggage, which consisted of a single suitcase had not arrived on the flight that I took from New York. The airline had promised to deliver it the next morning.

Thus, began my first night in the USA, going to sleep, at least partially hungry, and occupying a room, which I was not sure was mine to occupy and sleeping in the clothes in which I had travelled from halfway across the world.

7

THE JOURNEY BEGINS

Next morning (August 1), the first task was to report to the office of the Chief of Medicine. The Chief of Medicine was a very nice gentleman (Dr. Victor Grover). After the usual courteous exchange, he asked me how I pronounced my name. I said "Ved, pronounced Vaid, like paid or Vade, Gossai'n, n is half silent." He promptly said, "I think you better settle for Gosain," to which I readily agreed, not realizing the consequences (see below). I was just beginning my journey in the USA as a first-generation immigrant and did not know what to expect.

America is a land of immigrants. Thousands of people came here and continue to come here and there are innumerable success stories of those who have achieved the American Dream.

Many of the immigrants have gone on to win the Noble prize. However, it appears that achieving the "American dream" may be an exception rather than the rule.

According to Mary Sanchez, syndicated columnist Kansas City Star (2) as Published in Lansing State Journal, President Obama began his immigration speech with a lie. "My Fellow Americans, I would like to talk with you about immigration; our tradition of welcoming immigrants from around the world the president said to open his address". "Unfortunately, that is not quite true. We Americans love immigrant labor – the cheaper the better. But the immigrants themselves? Not so much. Here is how the game is played. We let immigrant labor in when it suits us, denounce it from the other side of our mouths for political advantage and then claim ignorance when it is pointed out that we have rigged the system for legal entry, so only a few can succeed. Beyond the labor, we do not welcome them as potential fellow citizens, not at first anyway. There has always been a cultural back lash – yes even to those past waves of Irish, Germans, Italians, Jews, and others. Among the first immigrant laws was the Chinese Exclusion Act, which aimed to halt immigration from that nation and to bar Chinese immigrants from re-entering the country if they left. This, after Chinese laborers helped build the rail roads. Scapegoating immigrants is a recurring theme in our nation's history. Laws were periodically passed in the late 19th and early 20th century to restrict Jews, Italians, Africans, and other Asians from legally coming to our shores. All of these immigrants did what immigrants do. They built their wealth, paid their taxes, contributed to economic growth and became solid citizens."

The physicians who immigrated to the US were no exception to these biased practices (See later). For those who immigrate, the process of acculturation and merging with the mainstream society is a difficult, complicated task which is also unique to every group of immigrants. The term "acculturation" was suggested as early as 1880 by John Wesley Powell to describe transformation of lifestyle and thinking of immigrants in their process of interaction with the insertion society. In 1936, Redfield and his collaborators considered acculturation as a cultural phenomenon defining it as a change in culture resulting from the contact between two distinct and independent cultural groups (Quoted by Cristina Ilie Ph.D. Candidate. (3)

America has also been called a "melting pot" but in recent times it appears more like a mosaic, where the immigrants do become part of the larger society but continue to maintain their culture and traditions. In general, immigrants go through at least 4 stages in the process of acculturation: (4)

1. Stage of shock
2. Stage of struggle

3. Stage of anxiety
4. Stage of settlement (or Stage of giving)

Physicians are no exception to this process, but their experiences may be unique because of their role as professionals.

The stage of shock begins almost as soon as the immigrant lands in the USA. My experience of hiring a cab to get to the hospital (see above) is but a small example of this.

The second example is, that I had accepted a different pronunciation of my last name as suggested by Dr. Grover. At the time, it appeared to be only a minor adjustment, but little did I realize at that time that with this change, I had lost my identity. That fact was brought home to me a few days later when a friend of mine called from New York and asked the hospital operator to page Dr. Gossai'n for him. The operator promptly replied, "We don't have a doctor with that name." My friend who was sure that I was a resident in that hospital insisted and said "let me spell his name for you G O S S A I N." The operator promptly replied "Yes! Of course, sir! Let me connect you to him." The irony of this small accommodation is that my children will not remember, and the grandchildren will not even know the correct pronunciation of their own last name.

The following night was my "on call" night. In the middle of the night, I was called about a patient who was having an acute attack of asthma and the nurse wanted to know what to do.

Me: "Please add 10 ml of Aminophylline (my pronunciation 'A my no phylline') in 100 ml of glucose saline and infuse over 10 minutes."

Nurse: "I am sorry Doctor I don't understand what you are saying."

I repeated the above instructions.

Nurse: "I am sorry Doctor. I don't understand what you are saying."

Me:	(Perplexed a bit, but I was confident) "It seems you have never heard of the medication that I am talking about."
Nurse:	"Yes! That is correct."
Me:	"Could I speak to the Nursing Supervisor please?"
Nurse:	"Yes, of course."
Nursing Supervisor:	"Yes, Doctor, can I help you?"
Me:	"I informed the Nursing supervisor, that I had given some instructions to infuse some 'A my no phylline', but she does not understand these and said she had never heard of this medication."
Nursing Supervisor:	"Yes! Doctor, I am afraid I don't understand it either."

Now I was really perplexed, particularly since I heard some laughter at the other end of the phone. Anecdotally, it may be noted that in those days (and to some extent even today) all foreign doctors were considered 'stupid' unless proven otherwise (emphasis is mine).

Fortunately, I was confident of what I was doing so I said, "Can I spell it for you?"

Nursing Supervisor: "Yes! Please do."

I spelled out AMINOPHYLLINE.

Nursing Supervisor: "Oh you mean 'AminOphlline'. No problem sir, we will take care of that."

I felt relieved and silently said "Thank God that I did not make a fool of myself."

The next morning when I went to the hospital ward, the head nurse of the unit came up to me and said "Doctor, will you spell your last name for me?"

Me: "G O S S A I N."

A few minutes later another nurse who was standing in the vicinity and I was sure that she had heard me spell my name, came up to me and said "Doctor, will you spell your last name for me."

Me: "G O S S A I N."

A few minutes later, another nurse who was also standing nearby and almost certainly had heard me spell my last name, came up to me and repeated the same question. I spelled it again for her 'G O S S A I N' but could not help but ask "What is going on here?" The three of them burst out laughing, making me wonder what I had done. A few moments later when the laughter had settled, the head nurse came up to me and said "We used to have another doctor from India. His name was 'Ramaswamy'. When we asked him to spell his name he would say "Y A R – Y E Y – Y U M YEY-YES-W-YEY-YUM-Y, and we used to have fun with that." I immediately recognized that Dr. Ramaswamy was from South India and probably had a heavy south Indian accent, common in that part of country, but I did not know at that time what to say, so I said nothing. Only later did I realize that these nurses were not only making fun of Dr. Ramaswamy's accent but were also looking for an opportunity for me to make the same mistake, so they could laugh at me as well. It was only much later that I felt sorry for them because these young ladies did not realize that anyone who speaks with an accent speaks at least one other language, which unfortunately most Americans do not. (This fact was highlighted by the famous comedian Johnny Carson, who once had an Italian guest who spoke with a very heavy accent.) When the audience laughed at his accent Johnny Carson reminded them that "Anyone who speaks English with an accent speaks at least one other language." He went on ask how many in the audience spoke another language, and not many hands went up.

A few days later, I was called to the intensive care unit (ICU) at night to see a patient who had arrived at the hospital in a state of coma (unconscious). Since the patient was seriously ill, the nurse, the head nurse, and the nursing supervisor, all had gathered around the patient's bed. As I began to examine the patient, I asked the nurse

"Can I have a torch please." Instead of getting a response, I had three young ladies staring at me with a clear look of profound surprise on their faces. The nurse said, "What do you want Doctor?" I said, "A torch please." The nurse, acting even more surprised said, "What are you going to do with a torch?" I said, "Look in his eyes to see the status of his pupils."

Nurse: "Oh! You need a flashlight. Yes! Of course."

Only later did I realize that the word torch, synonymous to me with a flashlight, probably meant to them that I was going to set the whole ICU on fire.

Another such example, which was related to me by a colleague, involved a female resident from India. Having recently arrived from India to begin her internship, she was dressed in her sari. She went to see a patient, a farmer, introduced herself and said "I am a doctor …. I am an intern. I will take your history and do a physical exam. I will then present my findings to my attending doctor, who is your doctor, and then we will come up with a plan for the management of your illness." The farmer replied "No way! Honey! you look pretty in your dress, but I will be damned if you are going to be my doctor." The poor thing, with tears in her eyes, quickly exited the room and later had to tell her attending why she could not examine the patient that was assigned to her.

Another example of "shock" that I experienced was that one night, I went to see a patient in the hospital in the middle of the night and when I came back to my room, I noticed that the lights were on although I was quite sure that I had turned the lights off. I also noted that the window had been propped open, while I was quite sure that the windows were closed because the weather was still slightly chilly. I opened the drawer of my desk only to discover that the cash amount in my wallet, all 50 dollars of it was gone. My salary in those days was $69.39 per week. I had cashed my first paycheck and had brought back 50 dollars which now had been stolen. I could not believe that in this land of opportunity such petty thefts would even occur. The image of America that I had at that time was that the roads were paved with gold and dollars were hanging on the trees that anyone could get. With improved communications and the advent of the internet, the incoming residents have a much clearer idea of what to expect when they arrive in the US. Nevertheless, I informed the hospital security, who informed me, in turn that such thefts were common, which was even more surprising, but an important lesson for me. He also assured me that although they would investigate the situation, it was very unlikely that the money would be recovered. It was not recovered.

I am sure others may have many other examples of their early experiences, which they might classify as "shock".

8

MY FIRST AMERICAN PARTY

About a month after my arrival in the USA there was a party to "welcome" the new house staff and also to say "goodbye" to those who had completed their training and were moving on to bigger and better things. (Although by this time, most of the graduating residents had left town.) In any event, it was a large gathering of people consisting of the attending physicians, the entire house staff and the staff that were involved in the business of the house staff. There must have been about 100-150 people at that party. Everybody was accompanied by their significant other or at least a date, except me. Interestingly, there also was a young, single, and pretty secretary who worked in the house staff office who was also not accompanied by a date.

Soon after the party started, there were drinks and music, so the people started to dance. My chief resident kept encouraging me to go ask this young lady named Darlene (but those who wanted to flirt with her called her Darlin) for a dance. I was too new to the environment, had never asked anyone for a date and simply did not have the courage to ask her for a dance. Incidentally, in those days the US immigration service used to publish a booklet with simple directions for the new immigrants, such as how to obtain social security card, a driver's license etc. Included in this book were also directions about how to ask a young lady for a date and it emphasized the fact that the morals of young women in America were no different than the women in your country of origin and may even be stricter. Nevertheless, it did go on to say that if you call a young lady for a date, you ask her "Mary, are you free on Friday night to go see a movie with me" and if she turns you down, don't take that necessarily a rejection, because she could indeed be busy that night. However, I had not had an opportunity to try that approach so far. So, at that point, my chief resident would say, "if you are not going to ask her for a dance, then have another drink." His constant "encouragement" to have another drink got me to the point of being intoxicated, such that I did ask her for a dance and danced with her. I have no idea what steps I was taking but one of the secretaries commented that at least I was keeping up with the music that was being played. Later, however, I got sick as a result of all that alcohol and learned my lesson about the limits of alcohol intake.

9

MY FIRST VISIT TO AN AMERICAN RESTAURANT

A few days after I had been in the US, my roommate (another fellow Indian) and his fiancé, a local Caucasian woman and a nurse, invited me to accompany them for dinner at a local restaurant, which was very famous for its steaks. I accepted the invitation, even though I was (and still am) basically a vegetarian. However, in the 1960's being a strict vegetarian in the USA was not easy. Most of the restaurants were not even aware that there were people who did not eat meat. If I informed the waiter in a restaurant that I was a vegetarian, and what could I have that was on their menu, the conversation went something like this:

"Do you eat Chicken? No; Do you eat Fish? No."

To most American waiters, and restaurants, at least in those days, not eating meat meant not eating beef. As a result of that, I had accepted the fact that I was going to have to eat meat to survive. Following this realization, I did eat meat on multiple occasions, including Steaks, Veal, Fish, and hamburgers etc. I did not even ask, what kind of meat I was eating. It was simply a matter of survival. However, for the last 25 years or so, I have given up eating beef for health and religious reasons.

Once at that restaurant, I was asked if I wanted my steak rare, medium, or well done.

Naturally, I opted for well done, even though I was informed that it was not the best way to enjoy a steak. I, on the other hand, wanted to make sure that the meat was well cooked. The size of the steak was also too big for me and I just could not finish it. At that point Helen (my friend's fiancé) asked me if I wanted a "doggy bag." I did not even know what a "doggy bag" was. So, Helen went on to explain that people take their left-over food with them and feed it to their dogs, although more and more people were using that food to eat themselves at a later time. Taking the leftover food from a restaurant home is not something commonly done back in India. So, I thought she was "pulling my leg" and consequently I said, "No, that is fine." She responded, "If you are too embarrassed to ask, I will ask them for you,". Just to find out what would happen, I responded "OK, go ahead" and she did. On our way out of the restaurant, I saw a long line of "doggy bags" sitting on the counter, with people's name on them for those who were taking their left-over food. It was another interesting lesson that I learned. These days, however, it has become customary to ask the waiter for a "box" in which to take the leftover food to be consumed later. The portion sizes of the food in American restaurants have also progressively increased in the recent past. Many physicians believe that the increased portion sizes may at least be partly responsible for the increased incidence of obesity in USA.

10

MY FIRST NEW YEAR PARTY

On the New Year's Eve, a nurse in our hospital and her husband had a "New Year party" at their house and I was invited too. I was glad to join them. There were quite a few people and plenty of food as well alcohol. By now, I had learned my tolerance for alcohol, so I had alcohol within my limit and was quite sober throughout and remained so till the end of the party. Several people were taking one more drink for the road (as was customary in those days) which I declined. I departed shortly after midnight. It was a cold wintery night and it had been snowing all evening, such that we had 3 to 4" of snow by then. I had hardly gone half a mile when my car got stuck in snow. It was an old car that I had purchased for $300. The salesman had given me the pitch, which I learned later was standard to "fool" guys like me, namely "the car was owned by an old lady and all she used it for, was to go to the church every Sunday". In any event, luckily for me, a black gentleman stopped by to help me. He asked if I had snow tires on my car. I had no idea that I was supposed to have put snow tires on the car. He then went on to emphasize that I must have snow tires if I wanted to continue to drive in that weather. He then asked if I had any chains in my car, and once again, I had no idea what he was talking about. At that point he pulled out a couple of chains from his car's trunk and put them on my car's tires and said, "Now You can drive home, and you should not have any trouble". When I asked him how and when I could return his chains, he responded, "Don't worry about it. You can return it to me any time." I took his phone number, thanked him profusely and left." I was really impressed and thought all Americans were this nice. I should add that things have changed dramatically over the years. Back in the old days, it was common for people to give rides to strangers, but now a days hardly anybody gives any rides to anyone. On the contrary, people are warned against giving rides to the strangers in case they may hurt you.

But gradually in a matter of a few days, but more like a few weeks or few months, the immigrants (myself included) begin to get used to the local vocabulary and local customs/traditions. The stage of shock begins to give place to the stage of struggle.

11

STAGE OF STRUGGLE

The state of struggle may also be called a stage of accommodation. In this stage, the immigrants begin to change themselves to "fit in" in the new culture that they have come into. They begin to change their pronunciation and alter their "accent", so that they can be more easily understood. For example, "caan't" becomes can't (kant) tamato to tomato. Zed (Z) becomes a Zee (Z). Instead of saying "I am going to do XYZ, they begin to say I am "gonna" do XYZ, and instead of saying "how are you doing?" they now say, "how you 'doin'?" etc. They also change their names to make it easier to assimilate and to make it look like that they are not foreigners. For example, Mukesh becomes Mike, Harish becomes Harry, Ashok becomes Ash, Sukhbir becomes Sue, and Anuja becomes Ann and so on.

Some of the names have been changed so much that it is not even possible to think of the original names. For example, Sathyan, became Seth and Kalpen Suresh became Kal Pen (now a famous actor) and so on.

They also start to change how they dress. It is generally not a problem for men who are by and large used to wearing "western clothes", but it may be a major change for some women particularly those from the Indian subcontinent. In the 1960's 1970's and 1980's, most Indian women would dress in a sari or outfits that would cover their legs all the way to their ankles. So, they found wearing skirts or dresses which would expose their legs below the knees, generally unacceptable. Luckily for them, right around that time the female nurses in the hospitals in the USA began wearing pant suits. This was a "God sent" for the female physicians from the Indian subcontinent. They rapidly took to wearing pant suits. Over the years, these women have accepted the western dresses and many immigrant women from India can now be seen in western dresses and even shorts. The dress code was not an issue for me since I was used to western dress any way. At this time many immigrants from India, myself included, also discover that although they are quite fluent in the English language, it is sometimes difficult to communicate, because the language spoken in this country is not the same English that they had learned. For example, one day I asked a nurse in the hospital, if I could get a lift from her. She looked at me with surprise and said, "what do you want". I responded "a lift" to go to downtown. She still was not quite clear as to what I was asking for. So, I repeated, when you finish your shift and go home, can I go with you in your car and will you drop me in downtown. She replied, "Oh you need a ride". No problem, I would be happy to give you a ride.

For physicians (and perhaps for other professionals), there is an additional problem, i.e., to prove their professional competency. As alluded to earlier, it was assumed that the training and competency of foreign physicians was inferior to the American trained physicians, unless proven otherwise

In the USA, the immigration of physicians from Asia began after 1965. In 1965, the Immigration and Nationality Act (PL89-236) abolished the national quota and gave preferences to individual occupations designated as "in short supply" by US Department of Labor. This law was approved by the congress during the Kennedy administration but was signed into law by President Johnson. Prior to that, immigration of Asians was not permitted. In the late 1960's and early 1970's, this new law led to a large number of physicians arriving in the USA, as they felt welcome. Many hospitals sent their representatives to foreign countries to recruit physicians and also offered to pay for their airfare or extended interest free loan to purchase air tickets. In the years 1970-71 the US immigration became even more liberal. They allowed all physicians regardless of their visa status, including J1 visa which has a requirement to return to the country of origin for at least two years before applying for permanent residency, to immediately apply for "green card" or permanent resident status. This may be, because the Vietnam war was still on and the US armed forces required physicians to serve in the armed forces. The physicians could be drafted into service until the age of 35 and most of the young physicians fell into that category. At this time, I was halfway through my Endocrinology Fellowship and as previously mentioned was planning to return to India after completion of the Fellowship. However, friends and colleagues encouraged me to apply for the green card, using the argument that if I wanted to return to India, having a green card would not prevent it. Consequently, I did apply for and was able to obtain a green card without having to go home to India, despite the fact I was on a J1 visa. As a matter of fact, we tried to delay getting a green card to avoid being drafted, but without success. Consequently, as soon as I obtained my permanent resident status (green card), I was classified as A1, meaning that I could have been called at any time. (By this time, I was married, and we had our daughter who was barely 4 months old). I tried to petition the Selective services, that we had no family in this country, and we had a small child and therefore I should be exempted, but that was of no avail.) However, fortunately, that did not happen, and I was able to finish my training without being drafted. The welcoming climate that International medical graduates (IMGs) had previously enjoyed in the United States began changing in mid 1970's. The Health Professional Educational Assistance act of 1976 (PL 94-484) declared an end to the physician shortage.

In early 1950's the immigration of foreign physicians had led to concerns over their command of English language and medical skills. A decision to test their readiness to undergo training was made by the leadership of medical organizations such as American Medical Association. (www.ecfmg.org). To test the competency of foreign medical graduates (FMGs) several tests were instituted. In 1958 the

ECFMG medical knowledge examination, known as the American Medical Qualification (AMQ) was introduced. In 1977 the Visa Qualifying Exam (VQE) developed by National Board of Medical Examiners (NBME) considered equivalent to NBME part I and II was introduced. In 1971 Federal Licensing Examination (FLEX) was accepted as an alternative pathway for IMGs to get licenses in different states. In 1992 United States Medical Licensing Examination (USMLE) step 1 and step 2 were introduced and in 1998 the ECFMG Clinical Skills Assessment (CSA) was introduced which was replaced by Clinical Skills examination (CS) in 2004. All these examinations were created to test the competency of the foreign medical graduates Even though, the IMGS were required to pass these examinations, their training and preparedness for entering a training program in the US was not considered equivalent to the US graduates. Numerous articles were written trying to establish that the foreign medical graduates (FMGs), later also known as International Medical Graduates (IMGs) were not as competent, as the US trained physicians based on their performance initially on the ECFMG exams and subsequently on VISA Qualifying Exams (VQE) and later even on FLEX and even more recently on USMLE (United States Medical License Exams) (5,6,7). To some extent the IMGs themselves pushed for these exams to be taken by the IMGs to prove that their qualifications and clinical skills were equivalent to the US MDs. It was argued that the success on a multiple-choice exam does not equate the clinical competence of a physician. Little did the authors of these articles, in my opinion, realized that for many of the FMGs multiple choice type exams was a new experience, and the fact that English was not their first language could easily explain at least in part, their lower performance on the exams mentioned above. We will never know how American trained physicians might do if they were asked to take essay type examination, which many foreign medical schools (including mine) required. There are anecdotal examples through which an American trained physician did not do so well when asked to see patients in a different environment. A story that I remember which was published in a magazine called "Resident Physician" which is no longer being published to my knowledge, described the experience of a Harvard trained physician when he visited India. This young physician after completing an Internal Medicine residency at Harvard went to visit All India Institute of Medical sciences (AIIMS) in New Delhi. He was invited to make rounds with the residents at AIIMS. He was presented a case of right upper quadrant pain, fever and enlarged liver. While he was thinking of viral hepatitis, hepatoma, (tumors of the liver) etc., the presenting intern informed him that it was a case of Amoebic liver abscess, and he had already aspirated a chocolate brown pus from that liver, thus establishing the diagnosis and instituting treatment at the same time, whereas the visiting physician had not even considered as one of the diagnostic possibilities.

When faced with another patient with cough, fever, and rales (abnormal sounds) in the upper part of right lung, he was thinking of lung cancer, lung abscess, only to be informed that the patient had tuberculosis, and he was already on treatment. To be at their best, a physician needs to be familiar with the local environment and to know what diseases are common in each area. I only relate this incident to indicate that when brought to a new environment, any physician will have some difficulty functioning comfortably and at his/her best

To be fair, there were other articles indicating that at least many FMGs were no less competent than US trained physicians (8,9,10) Nevertheless, FMGs continued to be discriminated against, sometimes subtly and sometimes not so subtly. Vibha Bhalla a professor at the Bowling Green University in Bowling Green Ohio states that in large measure, Indian FMGs considered questions about their competence a slanderous propaganda aimed to destroy their reputations and livelihoods. (11) A physician wrote in "India Abroad" "it is a fashion bordering on patriotism to look down upon FMGs"(12) He also stated that "when you need me, you send me a ticket to India, then you receive me at the airport, put me in a beautiful quarter, because you need me, and when I become a competition, you call me a problem." In the face of bias, Indian immigrant physicians in the metropolitan Detroit area decided to form an ethnic professional organization known as Michigan Association of Physicians of Indian Origin, which later became the American Association of Physicians of Indian origin (AAPI) to take collective action to fight discrimination. The association grew in numbers and some members introduced a resolution to form a section for FMGs in the American Medical Association (AMA) in 1981, which was soundly defeated. However, the struggle to establish a section for FMGs continued and section for IMGs was finally established in 1997 within the AMA. Today the AAPI claims to have more than 50, 000 members. The mission of the IMG section of AMA is to look after the interests of IMGs. The IMG section (of AMA) has continued to work diligently for the cause of IMGs. A great deal of discrimination has been removed but it still persists.(13) This is even though there are studies to document that hospitalized patients who receive care from IMGs had lower mortality than the patients treated by US graduates based on a study of more than a million hospital admissions.(14)

As recently as 2012, the President of AMA, when speaking to the Pakistani-American physicians, admitted that discrimination persists,

e.g., some states require only one year of training for USMGs to get a license where FMGs may require two or three years. (15) (At the time of this writing, there are still 35 states where the IMGs are required to complete additional years of training to obtain a license, compared to USMGs). This is even though the IMG section of AMA has written letters to each of these states to remove this discriminatory practice. In my own state of Michigan, until a few years ago, USMGs required only one year of training, whereas FMGs required two years of training to obtain a state license. The FMGs lobbied to the state licensing board and the rule was changed, such that all physicians now require two years of training to obtain an unrestricted license. One of the AMA presidents also noted that many residency programs require higher USMLE scores from FMGs compared to USMGs as a criterion for selecting candidates for interview. I believe that this practice is widespread, if for no other reason than simply the fact that many IMGs with very high scores on USMLE exams are readily available.

The governing council of IMGs (AMA) has published a paper delineating the role of IMGs in American Medicine. The details of that are beyond the scope of this chapter. Suffice to say, that at present, nearly 25% of American physicians are FMGs and nearly 27% of the residency positions in the USA are filled by FMGs. While majority of these foreign physicians obtain a J1 or an H Visa for training positions, about 75% end up staying in the USA. Those on J1 visas are required to go back to their country of origin for two years but they can get a waiver by agreeing to serve in underserved areas and many have used this avenue to continue to stay in the USA. Many FMGs have entered primary care specialties, as opposed to USMGs, who tend to enter more lucrative subspecialties such as dermatology, ophthalmology and orthopedic surgery and also have gone on to serve in areas where no American (USMG) wants to go.

It may be my biased viewpoint, but I believe that American medical system has used this avenue to solve the problem of physician shortage at least partly, predicted to be between 46,000 to 90,000 by the year 2025.(16) and the mal- distribution of physicians.

However, not all FMGs have taken this route and many have opted to take other career paths including a career in academic medicine, despite many difficulties encountered. Between 1981 and 2000, the number of FMGs in medical school faculties doubled from 8,100 to 16,200. However, in terms of percentage this number remains close to about 17-18%. (17) In my own case, anecdotally, the path to academic medicine, and success, thereafter, has not been an easy one. As mentioned earlier, I had arrived in the US as a second-year resident. After two years of residency, I applied to take the American Board of Internal Medicine (ABIM) exam, but the board denied that, arguing that I had only two years of Internal Medicine training, whereas three years were required. The board simply refused to recognize my three years of residency training in Internal Medicine in AIIMS and gave me no credit for that whatsoever. I might add that the ABIM continues to refuse to recognize any training in Internal Medicine obtained outside the US with few exceptions. Occasionally, the board will give credit for one year, on an individual basis, based on the recommendations of of the program director, or on the recommendation of the chairperson of the department of medicine of the medical school or if the individual has achieved the rank of an associate professor in a US medical school. I should add that for all practical purposes, it is difficult, if not impossible for a faculty member to achieve the rank of an associate professor in Internal Medicine without being certified by ABIM. This makes many well qualified physicians "trapped" and prevents many other eminent physicians from immigrating to USA.

Consequently, in my case, I approached the Chief of Medicine, as to what could I do to become "board eligible". He responded "Ved! I would have liked you to serve on the faculty but given the fact that ABIM wants you to do another year of training, why don't we appoint you as the "Chief Resident" and have you serve the role of a junior faculty" (Dr. William S. Frankl Chief of Medicine at Springfield Hospital Medical Center in 1969). By doing so, I became "board eligible." The year that I served as the chief resident also provided an opportunity to explore further, whether I wanted to continue on the path of Endocrinology or look for other subspecialties. The hospital had just started a Cardiac Cath lab and I was given an opportunity to rotate with the cardiology staff and to participate in some cardiac catheterization procedures. Many of my colleagues are surprised when I tell them that as a chief resident, I had done left heart catheterizations, a highly technical procedure. (In this procedure a tiny tube is inserted through an artery and into the heart to evaluate the function of the heart and the state of the coronary arteries. The procedure is typically performed by highly trained cardiologists). In those days, hospital staffs were also a great deal more liberal than they are today. In today's environment, I would not be allowed to place a catheter in the central vein, a procedure that is far more simple than left heart catheterization. Through the contacts of the chief of Medicine, I was provided an opportunity to rotate through the Endocrinology division at the Temple University medical school in Philadelphia where I spent three months. After spending three months in Cardiology at Springfield hospital and three months in Endocrinology at the Temple University, I was convinced that I wanted to be an Endocrinologist and not a Cardiologist. By now I had finally reached a point where it was possible to look for a fellowship in Endocrinology. After applying to several institutions, I was interviewed at the University of Cincinnati, Ohio. It is interesting to note that on the day of my interview, the program director of the Endocrinology (late Dr Harvey Knowles), who was also Chief of the division of Endocrinology, President of the American Diabetes association and the editor in chief of the journal "Diabetes", informed me that he had reviewed an article where I was a coauthor and had also accepted that for publication in the journal "Diabetes", a prestigious journal in the field of Diabetes. I would never know if that had anything to do with it, but I was offered and accepted a fellowship at the University of Cincinnati to begin on July 1. 1970.

The role of IMGs in American medicine seems established and is well recognized by the American establishment, as well as the FMGs themselves. The role of foreign-born physicians in the global health care has recently been emphasized in a recent article by Nwadiuko et al (18). They have emphasized that "when engaging productively in their homelands, foreign born IMGs have the potential of representing what the United states has to offer including its capacity for inclusion and willing ness to address important world challenges"(18). They further state that "Today's sociopolitical climate represents an opportunity for policy makers and medical educators to think critically about the shared benefits IMGs can provide to the United States and to their home countries"(18). The FMGs feel that they have contributed significantly (and continue to contribute) to the American healthcare system but also feel underappreciated and still discriminated against. However, the future of the incoming generations of IMGs appears to be insecure. Due to the predicted shortage of physicians in the future, several new medical schools have opened and some existing medical schools have increased their class size. However, the number of residency positions have remained the same. Unless the US Congress authorizes an increase in the number of residency spots, the FMGs will be squeezed out of the training spots. It is projected that the number of USMGs will exceed the residency spots in the very near future. In addition to the increase in the USMGS, several US citizens are now attending medical schools abroad, mainly in the Caribbean (They are US citizens but IMGs.) and returning to the US to compete for the residency spots. It is predicted that they will be given preference over the foreign-born physicians because of their familiarity with the US healthcare system and command of English language. However, only about 50% of the IMGS get matched for a residency position in the first year whether they are USIMGS or IMGS of foreign descent. Many of them carry an educational loan ranging from 200,000 to 300,000 dollars. This group of young physicians who have MD after their name but are not eligible to get a license to practice medicine should be a cause of great concern to the medical establishment in this country. However, there are no initiatives from organized medicine to address this problem. Everyone is left to his/her own devices to deal with the issue of not matching for a residency and thus having MD after their name and yet not be able to practice Medicine.

What happens to these US IMGS, who are unable to get a residency, and therefore not be able to practice medicine is largely unknown, because it has not been studied. There are anecdotal stories that many of them are working in nonmedical fields as unskilled workers, such as taxi drivers and waiters in restaurants.

12

GETTING MARRIED

By the time I was a chief resident, I was 29 years old, which according to my mother, was already past the age at which a young man should be married. Consequently, she was pressuring me to get married. Even before that, when I was first leaving India in 1967, she had wanted me to get married before I left for the USA, because she was afraid that I would marry a "White" girl, which in her mind was not acceptable. I must admit that I was lonely enough in my new environment that the thought of getting married had crossed my mind more than once. However, the question was should it be a "love marriage" or an "arranged marriage". Having grown up in India, where arranged marriages are common, I was leaning towards an arranged marriage. Although, the opportunity to know one's partner in love marriage was also an attractive as well as a viable option, but I had not run in to anyone that I would have considered having a long-time relationship with. My leaning towards an arranged marriage was in line with what most Indians prefer. According to a survey conducted by New Delhi TV (NDTV), in 2012, 74% Indians still prefer an arranged marriage (19). The merits and demerits of the two types of marriages have been discussed for a long time. In an arranged marriage, parents of the prospective brides and grooms select a potential partner, who comes from a similar socioeconomic background. In many instances, the two families have known each other for a generation or two.

In ancient times in India, the custom of child marriages was common. Therefore, it was evident that parents were able to select the "perfect" partner for their son or daughter. However, in recent times, the custom of child marriages has faded, but the tradition of arranged marriages remains quite prevalent.

Although arranged marriage has been considered an Eastern tradition, and love marriage a Western tradition, in olden times, arranged marriages were common among British Royalty.

For those who believe in an arranged marriage, marriage is considered not only a union between the two people getting married, but it is also a union of two families. The bride and groom become an integral part of the two families. In love marriages, there is much greater emphasis on the union of two people, sometimes even with no regard for each other's family. In such instances, integration into each other's family may be far more difficult.

In arranged marriages, two people make a promise to each other to make compromises with each other for the rest of their lives and make a commitment to each other until "death do us part". In love marriages on the other hand, the couples take their time to get to know each other, fall in love, sometimes even live together and then and only then, they get married. They figure that they know each other well enough and will have to make hardly any compromises in their married life. But such expectations may not fully work out because there are so many "bumps" that come along in marriage, and if the couple is not willing to make compromises every step of the way, that marriage is doomed to failure. In addition, in the case of an arranged marriage, the parents and family were much more involved before the marriage was solemnized. Therefore, in case a conflict arises in the marriage, the couple can turn to their parents for advice. More often than not, the conflict is resolved, and the couple moves on as a couple. In the case of a love marriage when a conflict arises, the couple is on their own and it is much harder to resolve the conflicts. In the Western world, where the love marriages are far more common, this has led to the development of marriage counselors. I believe that these professional counselors give the same advice that in case of an arranged marriage, the parents of the couple will, namely, find out what you are doing right and what the spouse is doing wrong, and also, find out the positives, discuss what compromises are needed and resolve the conflict. On top of it, the parental advice comes free, and with lots of love, whereas the professional advice is more businesslike and could be very expensive.

Whether arranged marriages produce loving respectful relationships is a question as old as the institution of marriage itself. In an era when 40 to 50 percent of all-American marriages end in divorce, some marriage experts are asking whether arranged marriages produce better relationships in the long run than do typical American marriages in which people find their partners on their own and romance is the foundation (20). By contrast, in Eastern countries where arranged marriages are more common the divorce rate is considerably lower. For example, the divorce rates in India are below 3% where divorce still carries a stigma. Although, still low, the divorce rates in South Korea, Iran and China are climbing. In 2001 the divorce rate in South Korea was 2.8 /1000 persons, which was above the European Union's average of 1.8 and Japan's 2.3 (21).

By another estimate the divorce rate in India is about 1%, compared to France (55%) Spain (65 %) and USA (46%) (22).

Robert Epstein, a senior research psychologist at the American Institute for Behavior and Research and Technology in Vista California, and author of a study "How love emerges in arranged marriages" (23), found that one key to a strong marriage is the amount of parental involvement at its start. The most important thing the parents of the couple do, he said, is to "screen for deal breakers".

"We celebrate autonomy" noted Dr. Epstein, which he explained, is why adult children bristle at the idea (quoted by Ji Hyun Lee (20). He also stated that he did not see arranged marriages becoming common in the USA.

Brian J Willoughby, an assistant professor in the school of Family Life at Brigham Young University said "Arranged marriages start cold and heat up and boil as the couple grows. Non arranged marriages are expected to start boiling but many eventually find that the heat dissipates, and we are left with a relationship that is cold" (Quoted by Ji Hyun Lee (20).

Over the years however, the complexities of both the arranged and love marriages have changed. The modern "arranged marriage", at least in India and among Indians, is that after the parents have done the initial screening, the couple is allowed (actually encouraged) to meet a few times over the next few days to few weeks (but not for a few months or years). This allows the couple an opportunity to get to know each other better and to determine for themselves if they can commit to spend the rest of their lives with each other. We might call this arranged/love marriage. On the other hand, if during this brief courtship, they find something unacceptable, the relationship does not proceed any further. One such incident happened in our own family, where my niece was introduced to a young man by her parents, who was otherwise found to be a very "suitable" young man for her. During their brief courtship, the young man said that he wanted his wife to be a "stay at home" wife so that when he leaves for office, she would prepare breakfast for him, and when he returned home from work, she would be waiting for him with the evening tea. (By the way, this was not an unusual expectation for the parents of both of them at that time). However, this was unacceptable to my niece, who was a highly educated professional. She decided to call off the relationship. Subsequently, she met a young man and married him, despite some resistance (but with eventual consent) from both sets of parents. She has been happily married to her present husband, who is equally well educated, for the last 40 years and is now the grandmother of several grandchildren.

Similarly, the love marriage scene has also changed. Very long courtships are commonplace. We should note that no matter how long the courtship is, both parties put their best foot forward and ignore many of the faults of the other person. Nowadays, when they feel confident that they are headed towards marriage, they may decide to live together for a variable length of time, sometimes against the wishes of their family. But as mentioned above, young people value their autonomy. They continue on this path. Both of our two sons went this route before getting married and at least until now they seem to be happily married. Couple of my nieces are currently living with their boyfriends and "testing the waters "to see if they eventually want to get married to the person they are dating. This would appear to be contradictory to our Indian Culture and values, which, by the way is becoming obsolete for Indians living in the USA.

The National Survey of Family Growth (NSFG) reported that in the years between 2006-2010, 48% of women cohabited with a partner compared to 34% of, women in 1995. Between 1995 and 2006-2010, the percentage of women who cohabited as a first union increased for all Hispanic and other race groups except for Asian women. In 2006-2010, 70% of women with less than high school diploma cohabited as first union compared with 47% o with a bachelor's degree or higher.

In these years (2006-2010), 40% of first premarital cohabitation among women transitioned to marriage by 3 years, 30% remained intact and 27% dissolved. Nearly 20% of women experienced a pregnancy in the first year of their first premarital cohabitation (24).

A question that may be asked is, does cohabitation lead to a more stable marriage? Data from the 2006-2008, National Survey of Family Growth reveals that a dichotomous indicator of premarital cohabitation was in fact not associated with marital instability among women and men. Among cohabiters, marital commitment prior to cohabitation (engagement or definite plans for marriage) was tied to lower hazards of marital instability among women but not men.(25). On the other hand, Dush, et al studied two cohorts, those that got married between the years 1964-1980 (when cohabitation was less common) and those married between1981-1997, when cohabitation was more common. Spouses of both cohorts who cohabitated before marriage reported poorer marital quality and greater marital instability (26).

Thus, it is not entirely clear, if the marriages where couples cohabit before marriage, are any more successful compared to marriages where the couples did not live together? It should also be mentioned that just like during the period of dating, the cohabiting couples probably, again, are at their best behavior. Anecdotally, one of my secretaries, who had been married three times by the age of 34 and was now living again with one of her ex-husbands, mentioned to me "Dr. Gossain, living with a man and being married to a man are two completely different things". I guess she knew the difference.

Finally, what is perplexing to me personally, is what are the couples living together waiting for? In some instances, there are even children between them. Are they afraid of making the relationship "legal" because it certainly appears that they have made the "moral commitment" of a marriage or are they afraid of making a commitment and find it easier to just live together? In my own case, I opted to return to India, hopefully to find a partner by the arranged/love marriage. I was introduced to this young woman (soon to be my wife), attractive enough for me by her physical appearance. She was a physician and had already subspecialized in Obstetrics and Gynecology. Our families had known each other for at least two generations. The two families had already made sure that there were no "deal breakers". In our brief courtship, I explained to her how life was going to be different in the USA. She was used to having one or two maid servants at home, and I explained to her that it would not be possible. We certainly would not be able to afford a maid servant, not with my salary as a resident (approximately $10,000 annually in those days). I also explained to her that I had already signed up for a fellowship in Endocrinology at the University of Cincinnati, and it was my plan to return to India after completion of the fellowship with which she readily agreed.

More importantly from her own professional career, I explained to her that she would have to be certified by The Educational Commission of Foreign Medical Graduates (ECFMG), which would require passing a "tough" exam. In addition, even though she had wanted to pursue Obstetrics and Gynecology (Ob/Gyn) as a career choice, it may not be easily possible because (I) A suitable residency spot may not be available for her, (ii) Because of the nature of the specialty (many emergency calls) and with no help available at home in the form of a family member or maids, she may not prefer to follow Ob/Gyn. She understood that and was willing to make alternative career choices.

Thus, there being no "deal breakers", we got married on May 25th, 1970, exactly 17 days after we had met, and this marriage lasted until death did do us part (more on that later).

13

FELLOWSHIP AND TRANSITION TO MICHIGAN STATE UNIVERSITY

I want to remind the reader that my life is still in the stage of "struggle". After marriage, we returned to Springfield, Massachusetts briefly and then moved to Cincinnati to begin a fellowship in Endocrinology, in July 1970.

While I was pursuing my fellowship, my wife was staying home and preparing for exams for her ECFMG certification. We thought that it might be a good time to start a family. However, mother nature was not being cooperative, and she simply did not conceive. After a year of trying, we thought it was appropriate to investigate the reasons behind that. Further evaluation led to some minor hormonal abnormalities. This led to a recommendation of the use of a drug called "clomiphene" to induce a pregnancy. The use of Clomiphene, promptly resulted in the expected outcome, i.e., a pregnancy.

However, these events were responsible for an emotional roller coaster. The first year being the year of despondence, namely a life without any children and the second with excitement of expecting and then having a child. From that time onwards, I have had a greater understanding of the emotional state of parents who are unable to have children of their own spontaneously and a greater understanding of why some couples go through procedures like in vitro fertilization or other modern means of conception at a great emotional and financial cost.

Our daughter was born in May 1972 and the Fellowship was completed on June 30 1972.

Now, that the original aim for coming to USA (An Endocrinology fellowship) was completed, it was time to decide whether to continue to stay in the USA or return to India. Although the American Board of Internal Medicine (ABIM) had now declared me "board eligible", meaning that I could take the board exam, but I had not taken the board exam so far. Thus, if I returned to India at this juncture, I would have no American credentials to show after an investment of 5 years of life. The J1 Visa that we were on, also was set to expire and that would require returning to India. However, the US Department of State and the immigration service decided around that time that physicians, no matter what kind of a visa they were on, could apply to get a green card immediately. Presumably, this was because of the doctor shortage at that time and the increased need for physicians because of the ongoing Vietnam War. As a result, we applied for a green card and the application was approved without much of a problem. This contrasts with the situation these days where many professionals including physicians are waiting to get their green card for as long as 20 years or even more. The other question that needed to be addressed was, that although we were now entitled to stay in the country for as long as we wanted, what would be the trajectory of my career. It had been my dream to become a professor of Medicine, back from the medical school days and therefore the path that I wanted to take was the path of "Academic Medicine".

Therefore, rather than find a place to enter private practice or simply do some moon lighting to earn money, I opted to accept another year of training as a research fellow at the medical college of Wisconsin in Milwaukee, Wisconsin. My mentor at that time (late Dr Harvey Knowles) also confirmed that this was a good approach commenting that, "An additional year of training while at this time may appear to be unnecessary will go a long way to help you in the academic career. This extra year would therefore be a good investment in your career". It was also becoming apparent to me, that I may end up staying in the USA, at least for a few more years. Consequently, I decided to take the FLEX exam to obtain a license. It is interesting to note that when I applied to take the FLEX exam the state board of Ohio said that I was not eligible to take the FLEX exam because my premedical basic science education was considered inadequate. It seemed strange that they would challenge the education that I had received before entering the medical school, even at the point that I had completed not only medical school but also a residency and had nearly competed fellowship. In any event, I had not mentioned to the Ohio board that I had also completed one year of Bachelor of Science (B.Sc.) degree course prior to entering medical school. However, on producing that certificate of B.Sc., the board allowed me to sit for the exam. To take the test, we (my wife and I) drove to Columbus Ohio, the night before since the exam was to begin at 8 AM the next morning. The exam itself lasted for 8 hours and, by the time it was over, it was already getting dark. On our way back to Cincinnati, even though our car was only two years old, it got overheated and the smoke was coming out of the engine. I pulled out of the highway and we both moved as far from the car as we could, because we thought that the car might explode any minute. Luckily, that did not happen but standing on the highway in the cold wintery December night, with a pregnant wife was not pleasant, to say the least. We must have waited for about 30 minutes when a police car stopped by. By this time the car had cooled down and the police officer assured me that it was safe to drive to the nearest gas station about half a mile away. We got our car repaired and we finally made it home late at night. I passed that exam without any problem and was able to obtain a license to practice medicine in the state of Ohio.

Now that I had a medical license, I could moonlight in some hospital, if I wanted to, to supplement my income as a resident or a fellow which was barely enough to make ends meet. However, I moonlighted only rarely, mainly because the fellowship responsibilities did not leave much time to moonlight and I didn't want to leave my wife alone at home during the night. The experience itself was also not rewarding.

One night when I was moonlighting, a patient admitted to the ICU had a massive heart attack and expired. His wife obviously was very upset and kept on saying" why didn't you perform a heart transplant to save him" I explained to her as best as I could that procedure like heart transplant were not so easily performed, but she apparently was not satisfied. She went on to file a malpractice lawsuit against the hospital, which of course included me as the physician who was involved in her husband's care in his final moments. The hospital lawyers defended the case, and the case was ultimately dismissed as one being without any merit, but until then it was a cause for anxiety for me. I relate this incident only to indicate that the lawsuits for malpractice of medicine are common in the USA and any one can file a lawsuit.

However, my struggles for getting on the path of an academic faculty were not over yet, despite, 3 years of Postgraduate training in India, 3 years of residency in Internal Medicine, in the US, 2-year fellowship in Endocrinology at University of Cincinnati an additional year of "research fellowship" at the Medical College of Wisconsin. When I was about to complete the 3rd year of fellowship, a junior faculty position in Endocrinology (Endocrine Hypertension) was advertised at UCLA, and I applied. Since I already had a couple of publications dealing with renin angiotensin system (a scientific area, very relevant to the advertised position), I considered myself to be a strong candidate for that position. However, instead of getting an interview, I got a letter from the professor (ironically, he, himself, was an IMG) stating that, "The road to academic medicine is long and tortuous, and if you want to continue on that road, we can offer you a fellowship". While I agreed with him that the road to academic success is long and tortuous, I could not see myself taking up another year of fellowship. Fortunately, I was able to secure a position at the VA hospital and St Louis University school of medicine as an Assistant Professor in the section of Endocrinology and had an opportunity to work with an eminent endocrinologist, the late, Dr. Thomas Frawley. After completing the fellowship in Milwaukee, we moved to St Louis to begin my job there. Thus, began my path in academic medicine (more on that later).

In the meantime, my wife had successfully completed the prerequisites for obtaining a residency position. For reasons mentioned earlier, she opted to pursue a residency in Pathology. In the meantime, we were blessed with two children, one daughter, who was born in Cincinnati, Ohio, and a son, who was born in Milwaukee, Wisconsin. I was beginning to feel that perhaps the "stage of struggle" was over and the path to future appeared smooth, but as the saying goes "Man proposes, God disposes", that was not to be the case.

I was feeling relieved, actually enthusiastic, that my academic career had begun and with opportunity to work with a famous, well established investigator, the success was therefore almost assured, but that was not to be. At the time of my recruitment, Dr. Frawley had informed me that he was going to step down as the Chair of the Department of Medicine at St. Louis University School of Medicine and begin a new phase of his career as the "Distinguished Investigator of the Veterans Administration (VA)". The VA was going to build a laboratory for him, and he would have unrestricted access to $500,000 annually for research, a very handsome amount in those days. Besides me, he had also recruited two or three additional young

endocrinologists to be part of his "team". However, for a variety of reasons, including the bureaucracy of the VA, the details of which are not available to me, this plan did not work out and Dr Frawley did not accept the position at the VA. A couple of other young investigators, who had been recruited by him, got the wind of this much earlier than I did (since they were local), and they found alternative positions.

Soon after my arrival in St. Louis, I found myself in a nonexistent Endocrinology Section at the VA, and I began to look for alternative position.

While I find it easy to understand now, at that time, the bureaucracy in the VA hospital appeared unbelievable. As promised at the time of my recruitment, the hospital did provide me a laboratory space but that is all. I wasn't told (and I was naïve enough that I did not know) that to carry out any investigation in the laboratory, I would need to apply for funding from the VA, which would be available on a competitive basis only. Some furniture for the laboratory was also promised, but it appeared to me, that to move the furniture from storage to my laboratory would require an act of congress. I also became aware of "job description" of various employees. In those days, we routinely used to request reprints from the authors of the articles of interest. The reprint request was made by sending a card to the authors. I kept on giving my requests to the secretary of the department for about 3 months, but no reprints were arriving. So, one day I asked her why I was not receiving any reprints. She replied, "Because I have not been sending any cards out".

Me: How come?
She: It is not in my job description.
Me: I wish you had told me when I gave you those cards so I could have sent them myself.
She: Well! That is what you are going to have to do if you want those reprints.

My frustration must have been visible. So, one day an older VA physician took me aside, put his hand on my shoulder and said "young man! This is how VA works. If you don't like it, you should leave soon or get used to it. It is actually not so bad. I go to the wards every morning to make 'rounds' which takes me all of ten minutes and the rest of the day is mine for whatever, I may choose to do. I have been here for 37 years, and I am looking forward to my pension so I can retire." Although recently the health care at the VA hospitals has come under a great deal of criticism, I do not mean to imply that VA physicians are lazy or incompetent. Nevertheless, this further consolidated my desire to leave that situation and find an alternative academic appointment. I therefore, began to actively look for another opportunity.

However, before I left St Louis MO, Dr Frawley was also responsible for a recognition that I had so badly wanted at that time in my career, namely a fellowship in the American College of Physicians (FACP). One day, I received a call from Dr Frawley who also served as the governor of the American College of Physicians (ACP) for the state of Missouri informing me that the American college of physicians wanted to bestow the fellowship on me at the time of my initial application. Apparently, it was (and still is) somewhat unusual to get FACP at the time of first application. One needs to be a member of ACP for about two years, have some additional publications or other important contributions and then apply for the FACP. I was delighted to have this recognition because I valued the FACP very much and still do. Later, I was fortunate enough to receive the mastership from the college (MACP) in the year 2014.

It was around that time (June 1974) that I ran into David Rovner, MD. He had left the University of Michigan after several years to join Michigan State University's new Medical school. He in essence was the chief of the division of endocrinology and the section of Endocrinology, although the sections were not yet formalized at Michigan State University. We met at one of the Endocrine Society meetings, and he invited me to visit a newly established medical school in East Lansing, Michigan (College of Human Medicine). The dean of the medical school had arrived in 1964, the chair of the department of Medicine arrived in 1967 and the first class graduated in 1972. The college was new, not only in terms of the years that it had been in existence, but also in concept. It was one of the first "community based medical schools" in the country. The concept was that practicing physicians based in the community could teach young medical students and all they needed to know was how to practice medicine. There was no "University Hospital" (There still is not). Since a large amount of teaching was to be done by the volunteer faculty in town, there were only a few physicians that made up the so called "full time" teaching faculty.

It was risky for a young person aspiring for a successful academic career. However, I agreed to take that risk after the following incident. While I was being recruited, I asked an older well-established faculty member, why he had left an established tenured faculty position at an established medical school to come to this new "community based medical school". He replied, "Young man! That is a good question and initially I did not want to come either, but I changed my mind when the Chair of the Department, who also had left the same medical school said, "George! When in your life are you going to get a chance to participate in the development and shaping of a medical school?" It sounded interesting and challenging. During the interview process I also met a professor of Urology who had nothing positive to say about the medical school or its relationship with the community hospital where most of the medical education was supposed to take place. I later found out that he was in the process of leaving this place. I would never know if he was leaving of his own accord or was being asked to leave. Although, I was still somewhat apprehensive, I also found the situation challenging and intriguing. I accepted the position as an Assistant Professor in Medicine.

I must have impressed many faculty members who interviewed me including the Chief of Endocrinology (Dr Rovner) to have received the job offer, because it was many years later that I learned that the chair of the Department of Medicine was not in favor of hiring a foreign medical graduate, again reflecting the commonly held belief at that time, that the training and skills of the FMGs were not as good as US Medical graduates. However, after I had been in East Lansing for a few years and promoted to the level of Associate professor with tenure, he did congratulate me for having a successful academic career and added that, "I knew Dr Frawley's recommendation could not go wrong" (I guess, he and Dr Frawley were friends, both being chairmen of their departments). Although, I had requested that my present employer (St Louis University) not be contacted, apparently, he had spoken to Dr Frawley about me before I was invited for my second interview at MSU. I thanked him for his nice comments.

I joined the Department of Medicine at Michigan State University in April 1975. My wife also found a residency in Pathology in one of the local hospitals, and it appeared that the careers of both of us were on the right track, and we could look forward to a satisfying, if not bright future. But that was not to be, because fate had other plans for us. As we left St. Louis, Missouri, it was warm and sunny, but only a few miles before arriving in East Lansing, we were hit by a snowstorm. We lost our way and could not find the hotel where we had made reservations to stay until we could move into the apartment that we had rented. We ended up staying in another hotel. It never occurred to me at that time if this was a sign of worse things to come.

About two weeks later around April 14, another snowstorm hit the area. As I was getting ready to go to work, I looked outside, and all I could see was snow. I wondered if it was even safe to get out of the house and drive to work and then the radio announced, it has already snowed 15" and MSU has been closed for the first time in 50 years. That was a relief in that I did not have to go to work on that day, but if God was sending us messages about the things yet to come, we did not see it that way.

It has been mentioned before that about 75% of FMGs who came to this country ended up staying here. Let us examine why? I am not aware of the reasons for FMGs of all countries, but almost all the FMGs who arrived from India had planned to spend 3 to 5 years in the USA, complete a fellowship of their choice and return to India with this added expertise.

Again, I am not sure, if all the reasons for their stay have been investigated, but it appears that most of the physicians from India have simply "drifted" into careers of their choice in USA. Once the residencies or fellowships were completed, many of them wanted to return to India and find faculty positions in one of the medical schools in India or practice "state of the art" medicine in their own specialty. Unfortunately, the faculty positions would be hard to get because people who had stayed back would now have seniority and since most of the medical schools in those days were government institutions, it would be hard, if not impossible, to bypass seniority. For those who wanted to practice, they would not find adequate facilities, e.g., a cardiologist trained in invasive cardiology may not find a cardiac catheterization laboratory; a neurologist may not have found adequate facilities to perform EEG and EMG; an endocrinologist may not have found adequate laboratory support to provide meaningful care in endocrinology. Thus, many of us got over trained to practice or work in India. Moreover, after the completion of the training period there were plenty of opportunities in America which the individuals grabbed, whether it was private practice or an academic position. Many, if not most of us grabbed those opportunities, rather than go back to India and face an uncertain future.

The question, whether we made the right decision to stay in America still comes to my mind at times, enough that I have partnered with a social scientist to do a survey among Indian physicians, to seek answer to this very question. (more on it later).

14

DISASTER STRIKES

By this time (June 1975), we had moved into our new and first house. This may not have been a "dream house" but certainly was a house that we liked.

I still remember distinctly it was about December 20, 1975, a cold wintery night. It was snowing outside and the light reflecting from the snow was giving it a beautiful appearance. We had put both the kids to bed in their respective bedrooms, and both of us were sitting in the family room. The night was cold, so we had lit the fire, the crackling of the wood burning was adding a touch that was as soothing as a soothing background music.

I said to my wife, "We have two beautiful children, a nice house, I have a job that I like, and you have a residency position, which you will finish in another 3 years to become a pathologist. The future looks good. The Lord has finally been good to us." And she agreed. Little did we know that things were about to change in such a way that we had never imagined.

The next morning, she got up and said, "I think I have a urinary tract infection". I got up several times to go to the bathroom during the night and it has been hurting to urinate." I jokingly responded, "Most young women get urinary tract infections on their honeymoon or shortly thereafter. How come you are getting it now?" It was a Saturday morning, and I still took diligent care, as any doctor would have, if she had gone to see her primary care physician. I went to the lab, got a container for urinalysis (urine test) obtained a urine specimen from her, took it back to the lab, ordered a urinalysis including a culture if indicated, and prescribed an antibiotic for her. It was only a urinary tract infection, a rather common malady among young women, and there was no cause for concern. Symptomatically, she was better in a couple of days.

Approximately a month later, she got up in the morning and said, "My throat hurts, and it is even difficult for me to swallow my own saliva." I looked in her throat and was horrified. Both the tonsils were so enlarged that they had met in the midline, blocking almost the entire pharynx (throat). I said to myself, "no wonder she cannot swallow her own saliva". I was scared and had this sinking feeling in my heart that something serious was going on. We obviously needed to do something, but it was a weekend. Rather than run to the emergency room, I decided to call a colleague (Dr Robert Holmes an ENT surgeon, now deceased), who also happened to live in the neighborhood. Fortunately, he picked up the phone and said, "I will come over to your house and see her," but then he said "No! On a second thought, it would be better if you bring her to my office. I will open up the office for you, and there I will have all the equipment I will need to examine her." Anecdotally and somewhat sadly, I might add, that this type of collegiality and the willingness to go the extra step for a colleague in need, is a thing of the past. In the next few minutes, we all were headed to his office.

He took one look at her and said, "She has a serious throat infection. She is not able to swallow anything. We will have to give her fluids by vein (IV). Otherwise, she will get dehydrated. We could start an IV at your house if you like, but I think it would be better if we admit her to the hospital." I thought for a moment and wondered, what was I going to do with the kids if she goes to the hospital, but then I said to him, "We physicians often cut corners when it comes to taking care of our own health." I was scared enough that I said, OK, go ahead and admit her to the hospital, and I will manage the kids somehow.

He called me next morning and asked if she had been complaining of feeling weak or lack of energy or had there been a history of blood loss? I said, why you are asking all these questions to which he replied, "She is anemic. Her hemoglobin is only 8.6 gm/dl. (Normal is 12 to 14 gms /dl) You better ask someone from your department (a hematologist) to see her.", which I promptly did.

She was seen by an eminent hematologist, which we were fortunate to have in our own department at that time (Dr. Anthony Bowdler), who proceeded methodically to investigate the cause of her anemia. It is interesting to note that Dr Bowdler was a British physician, originally trained in the UK and had immigrated to the USA a few years earlier. The rumor has it, that he used to conduct experiments on himself for which he had his blood drawn multiple times. When he applied to get a Visa to the USA, people in the US embassy thought that he was a drug addict. He had to convince the immigration service that, that was not the case and he was able to get his immigration.

He asked her the usual questions that doctors ask young women when they are anemic. The answers to all those questions were of course negative. He considered several possibilities that could explain the symptoms that she was having and the results of her blood tests. After due consideration, he decided that although possible, Heme malignancy (Blood cancer) was not very likely in the presence of adequate platelets, the absence of normoblastemia (Abnormal blood cells) with no bone pain and neither lymphadenopathy (enlarged lymph nodes) or hepatosplenomegaly (enlarged liver or spleen).

It was reassuring that a hematological malignancy (blood cancer) was unlikely. He advised to initiate further investigations before deciding on bone marrow examination, which might prove necessary if clear directions did not emerge in the next few days.

Along with the sore throat, she had also developed a left upper lobe pneumonia (pneumonia in the upper part of left lung). A protein electrophoresis (a specialized blood test) was performed, which simply showed that it was consistent with an acute disease process. This test would be abnormal in anyone who is ill. On Feb 4/1976, hemoglobin had further dropped, and it might now require blood transfusion. Therefore, it seemed wise at this point to have a bone marrow examination before the blood picture was altered by the red blood cells given as part of the blood transfusion.

Three or four days went by and although her throat was getting better, we had no answer as to the cause of her anemia. So, one day, she said to me, "Maybe I have leukemia". Although, I immediately said, "What are you talking about? No way! Don't even think about it." Simultaneously, I missed a heartbeat and said to myself, "What if she really does? It is possible after all." Later, the same day, Dr. Bowdler approached both of us and said, "We have not been able to find a cause of her anemia. I think we should obtain a sample of her bone marrow."

Although, both of us were now really scared, we also knew, that was the right thing to do. Naturally, we gave our consent to him to perform the bone marrow. A bone marrow test was performed on February 5, 1976.

The results of the bone marrow were available the following day. I was at her bedside when Dr. Bowdler approached us. He sat down on the bed and said, "I have personally looked at the bone marrow slides. The marrow is very cellular. The cells are in the different stages of development, and there are many more immature cells than we expect to see in a normal marrow specimen." I responded somewhat scared and excited "Tony, you are telling me she has leukemia?" Dr. Bowdler said, "I am afraid so Ved!"

Those few words felt as if the weight of the whole universe had fallen on my head. My wife did not say a word, but I could see the fear of death in her eyes (A diagnosis of leukemia was literally a death sentence in those days). Dr. Bowdler remained seated on the edge of her bed for a few more minutes and then I asked him "What next?!" He calmly replied, "I will leave the two of you alone to absorb this, and we will discuss what to do next later on." As soon as he left, we hugged each other and cried. I held her close, as if holding her close would make her get better. Although it did not make the disease any less serious, it did make both of us feel better. It is hard to say, if she needed me more than I needed her, but I do remember feeling "I cannot let you go. I will die without you". When the tears stopped,

I said to her, "We are going to beat this. You will have to be brave and tolerate the chemotherapy or whatever else they throw at us." Simultaneously, I was thinking in my own mind, what if they are wrong and the pathologist, as well as Dr. Bowdler, had simply not interpreted the slides correctly?

I got a copy of the pathology report and retreated to the hospital's library and began looking at articles, which described the differential diagnosis of the cytological picture described in the bone marrow report. (That is what else, other disease state, other than the blood cancer could explain the reaction they were seeing in the cells of her bone marrow).

Leukemoid reaction (presence of abnormal cells without that being Leukemia) was clearly a possibility, but there was no history of an overwhelming infection, other than the recent urinary tract infection, and the respiratory infection (Sore throat and Pneumonia) that she had developed (Rarely, an overwhelming infection can cause a leukemoid reaction). Rarely tuberculosis could also present a picture like that, but again, there was no history of a recent tuberculosis. After spending almost the entire day in the library, I could not come up with an alternative explanation for the pathology report.

I felt I had to give up and accept, that the diagnosis of leukemia was indeed correct. That night, I gathered my two children and told them "we are going to pray". As I took them to the small closet where we had created a "temple" (almost every Hindu home has a temple), I began to wonder what we are going to say in our prayers. Although we had taken our children to a temple in Detroit, Michigan, I was not sure if they could recite any mantras in Sanskrit, and moreover, even if they could, would they understand what we were praying for? It was obvious that we (mainly me) had to create a prayer, which was meaningful to them. So, I did, and it went something like this "God! Thank you for a nice day. Thank you for everything else. Please make my mommy well so she can come home". Before I could finish saying the last few words, I began to cry, and tears were rolling down my cheeks. Watching this, my daughter, only 3 years old at that time, said "Daddy! Why are you crying?" I wanted to tell her "Because I am afraid that mommy may not come home at all", but those words simply would not come out of my mouth. (It is a bad omen to say things which are not pleasant, lest they turn out to be true, according to Hindu beliefs.) So instead of saying that, I said "Because Mommy is very ill, and we want her to come home and be with us". Although it has been several years since we began this ritual, and the kids, now grown-up adults probably don't even remember, I still recite a modified version of that prayer almost every day at about dinner time.

Next morning, I was back at the hospital early to meet Dr. Bowdler, having reconciled with his diagnosis, and prepared to give my consent along with my wife's to begin chemotherapy. However, when Dr. Bowdler arrived, and before he could tell us what his plans were for her treatment, I don't know where I got courage, but I said to him "Dr. Bowdler, what if you are wrong?" I was surprised at myself for having said so, because I was only a young physician and I was challenging a very eminent and experienced hematologist for whom a diagnosis of leukemia was as routine as making a diagnosis of diabetes or hyperthyroidism (overactive Thyroid) was for me. He, on the other hand, in his usual calm manner replied "Ved! Nothing would give me more pleasure than to be wrong in this instance, but I am afraid that I am not wrong". I don't know if I felt relieved or became more despondent at his response because the last bit of defense that I had, against the fact that my wife was suffering from leukemia had just come down. He, however, went on to say, "Would you like a second opinion?" Of course, I could not or would not refuse. He suggested that he would ask Dr. Scott Swisher, another eminent hematologist, who also happened to be a member of our department. He further said that we should not wait for his answer but proceed with the chemotherapy. Although he agreed that there was a very small chance of this being a leukemoid reaction, it will be an unsafe assumption, if acute myeloid leukemia (AML) is present and the chemotherapy is delayed. He, therefore, advised administration of frozen packed red blood cells and granulocyte (White blood cells) infusion to prepare her for chemotherapy with Adriamycin and Cytosine Arabinose (Drugs used to treat Leukemia).

She received her first dose of Adriamycin the following day (February 7th, 1976). Two days later, she was feeling nauseated, uncomfortable, and depressed. Who would not be depressed when told about a diagnosis of leukemia and undergoing chemotherapy? I don't know if I was more depressed than her, but I certainly was scared. It was difficult and painful to see her feeling this way and yet, I had to put up a brave front that it was going to be alright, and that the chemotherapy, although uncomfortable, and associated with several side effects (undesirable effects) along the way, was our only hope. Along with it, most likely because she was not eating, particularly not taking oral fluids, she began to develop electrolyte abnormalities (low sodium, low potassium in her blood), and the electrocardiogram (ECG) began to show nonspecific abnormalities of ST and T waves (Changes on the ECG that something may be wrong with her sodium or potassium or heart). Although these abnormalities may appear to be trivial to a lay person, and although her physicians were constantly reassuring us that everything was ok, I could not help but think that everything was not ok. Many non-physicians may think that when physicians themselves are patients, they have an advantage in that they understand the disease process and the need for whatever treatment is being prescribed. However, the opposite is usually true, and our case was no exception. As mentioned above, although the abnormalities may appear trivial, I would think of the worst possible complications of these abnormalities. for example, do the nonspecific 'T' waves mean she is developing myocarditis (damage to heart), as a result of the drugs, and was this going to lead to myocardial failure (failure of the function of the heart muscle) even before the chemotherapy could have any effect on the underlying leukemia or was the low potassium low enough that it could cause an arrhythmia (abnormal rhythm of the heart) which in its own right could be fatal without an extensive damage to the heart muscle. In our case, although we were both physicians, she had a background in Ob/Gyn and was now pursuing a pathology residency; I was an Internist (Endocrinologist), neither of us was an expert in treating leukemia. In her mind, because I was an Internist, I was supposed to know everything that was going on with her. So, although her physicians would take the time to explain everything to her, after their visit, she would turn to me and ask, "Will you tell me what Dr. Bowdler, or Dr. Campbell said?" At this point, I would have to re-explain everything back to her, but I would make sure that I emphasized the positives and minimized the negatives. However, every time I did that, I felt guilty that I was not telling her the whole truth. At the same time, I would say to myself, I must encourage her, so she would be able to cope with everything that was being thrown at her, such as blood transfusions, chemotherapy, antibiotics, and even parenteral nutrition (nutrition by vein). At the same time, I would be scared, that, what if all the complications I am not telling her turned out to be true? I knew, it was selfish of me to think that way, but at times, I felt that she had me for support, but who did I have for support? I needed to be strong for her and for our kids, who could only perceive that something was wrong because mommy was not home, but they had no idea of the seriousness of the situation. I also had to continue with my job at work. During the day, whenever I could, I would sneak out from work to be with her as much as I could. If I could not be there when her physicians would come to see her, I would catch them at work and get an update on her condition. I would come home exhausted, gather my kids, feed them dinner, say the prayer that we had created and put them to bed. After that, I would go to my bedroom, which felt so lonely without her, try to go to sleep, but lay awake for hours wondering what tomorrow was going to bring. The other complication that we still had to deal with was the Pneumonia. It had been suggested that we use postural drainage (change of position to loosen up her secretions) so that the lungs can clear up, but she was not able to tolerate that. Dr. Murphy (an infectious disease specialist) also saw her that day and he noted that she had a new splinter hemorrhage (tiny hemorrhage under the nails) an S3 gallop (an abnormal heart sound) and tachycardia (rapid heart rate). Although he did not say it in his notes, I knew that it implied that she may be developing (or had developed) subacute bacterial endocarditis (SBE) (A serious, frequently fatal infection of the lining of the heart). This new development was one more thing for me to worry about, but blood cultures were negative so far, making SBE somewhat less likely. Nevertheless, Dr. Bowdler began Digoxin (heart medication) to prevent her from going into congestive heart failure (failure of the pumping function of the heart).

She continued to run fever and had developed bulbous (big blister) lesions on her ear. While her doctors discussed differential diagnosis of her condition, most of which I comprehended but I was not interested in the academic discussions. I was most concerned about how this was going to affect her recovery and prognosis (future outcome). They talked about the possibilities of viruses (herpes) and fungal infections, and I was scared because these infections were far more difficult to treat than the usual bacterial infections, but people with underlying compromised immune system, such as those with Leukemia, do not develop "usual" infections. They develop infections which are unusual such as viral or fungal infections. I derived some satisfaction from the fact that at least so far, the AFB smear (diagnostic test for tuberculosis) was negative. They had aspirated the fluid from the bullous lesions and although the smears were negative for any bacteria, the culture had grown some gram-negative bacteria, which are sensitive to ampicillin and chloramphenicol (antibiotics to treat some infections). While they contemplated their next step, all I could think of was that they would start her on chloramphenicol (a very strong antibiotic which can further suppress the bone marrow and thereby limit recovery) and whatever chance her bone marrow had to recover would be wiped out. However, I had faith in her doctors, almost all of whom were my colleagues. Fortunately, I had a great deal of faith in the clinical judgment of Dr. Bowdler, who also happened to be the leader of the team. I was confident that he would weigh the risks and benefits of any steps taken and would not proceed with anything that appeared to be too risky. In his notes that day, Dr. Bowdler wrote "veins are becoming a limiting factor". She had been poked a thousand times, and all her veins were either thrombosed (blocked by blood clots) or collapsed. While her physicians were thinking of alternative strategies, all I could think of was that we would not be able to administer the chemotherapy that was needed. It seemed like a paradox that although we knew what to administer, we had no means to do that. I was scared, but I didn't know who to share my fears with. Her doctors were reassuring, but for them, she was just another patient. I saw my life slipping away. I could not share this with my children. They were too young to comprehend the seriousness of the situation, and for them, I had to maintain my composure and pretend that everything was under control and mommy would be home soon. We continued our routine of prayers before we went to bed. Almost every night they asked me "when is mommy going to be home", to which I responded, "I don't know beta (child) but hopefully soon". Although I said this almost reflexively, every time I said this, I missed a heartbeat, which told me what if this is not so?

I went to the hospital as often as I could and tried to be with her for as long a time as I could. I was still working full time and had my professional obligations to fulfill. I asked her how she was feeling, and she would say "I am fine but just a little tired". I would ask her just a little tired! That is all? Tired of being in the hospital! She would say that too, but they are giving me all these "poisons", which I think are making me tired. She would then turn around and ask me how I was doing, and I would say "I am fine".

Veena: "How are you coping with the job, and how are the kids?"
Me: "I am fine. People at work are very understanding. Kids are usually busy in school during the day, but every night they ask me when you are coming home. Honey! Please be strong and put up with this. We need you back home.

It was almost two weeks since the time that she had been hospitalized. She continued to spike temperature frequently. She was nauseated and vomited frequently and obviously looked exhausted, but she had not complained. She seemed to be accepting things as they came. I don't know where she derived the strength to tolerate what I think had been a physical and mental torture. I wondered frequently, how I would have reacted under similar circumstances? I would have probably collapsed by then. I thought it had been too long, and we hadn't made any progress. Little did I realize at that time that, that we still had a long road ahead.

Next, the resident on the ID service (Infectious Diseases) wrote in his note that systemic candidiasis (Generalized fungal infection) was a possibility. I could not say that he was wrong, but I was hoping that he was wrong, because systemic candidiasis, at least in my mind, would be difficult, if not impossible, to overcome. Also following the above note was a note by Dr. Campbell (one of the hematologists), "We are at a 'critical point' in this patient's course". She is experiencing the maximum effects of antineoplastic agents (Anticancer medications) as well as her other related conditions. He noticed that she was depressed. I took his note to mean this was the end of the road. If she did not respond to the chemotherapy, we would have nothing more to offer. However, he noted that "we will plan on granulocyte infusions".

A repeat bone marrow was performed (Feb,17) and a review of that revealed "a 40% decrease in cellularity, fewer pre normoblasts (Immature cells) were seen. This was the kind of response one anticipates at this time." I took this to be a hopeful sign, and I shared that with her. I tried to reassure her and myself that perhaps we would overcome this after all.

It had now nearly been a month that she had been in the hospital. She continued to complain of being nauseated, frequently throwing up, and the vomit was blood tinged. The fever had not resolved. To find out the cause of fever, all antibiotics were stopped to exclude the possibility of "drug fever". (Sometimes the antibiotics themselves can be the cause of the fever.) She, however, did not become afebrile (i.e., fever had not come down) after the discontinuation of antibiotics. To make matters more complicated, her liver functions had deteriorated to the point that her bilirubin was up to 9.4 mg/dl, and the liver enzymes were also elevated (These are signs of a failing liver). No one was sure what was causing this, but everyone was concerned. The options to change course as far as changing the medication were limited. So, we proceeded cautiously and followed the course of "watchful waiting".

There seemed to be no end of complications. Besides all the medical complications, she appeared to be confused that day (March,1/1976). Although I was trying to put up a bold face, telling her and myself that everything would be alright, I was scared to bring it up. I suspected that with all the infections she had, perhaps she also had a CNS (central nervous system such as brain) infection. My anxiety must have been obvious because one of the nurses wrote in her notes "husband appears quite anxious about lethargy and confusion today". I asked her how she was feeling, and she responded, "I am ok", but she was obviously short of breath and seemed to be having some discomfort while breathing. She finally did say that it hurts to take a deep breath.

A drowning man looks for anything he can hold onto. The first ray of hope appeared in the notes of Dr. Murphy "(March 7, 1976)." Bone marrow is beginning to respond. It seems that patient has responded to infections almost as well as some respond with normal white cells. Thanks to the white blood cells transfusions, which have been lifesaving so far, I believe it is time to be guardedly optimistic". My hopes were up, but clearly, we were not out of the woods yet.

Her skin complexion had become quite dark, and I brought up the possibility of adrenal insufficiency (failing adrenal glands, within my specialty after all). She was seen by my colleague, and he advised that we add steroids. (Medications used to treat deficiency of adrenal glands) That seemed "reasonable", but steroids could be a double-edged sword in view of the co-existing infections, (because they can make the infections worse and more difficult to treat.)

Blood tests showed hypoalbuminemia (low albumin), hypocalcemia (low calcium) and she remained jaundiced (bilirubin down from 9.4 to 7.4). Albumin was 2.4 gm/dl and calcium level were 6.4 mg/dl (both the albumin and calcium were too low). Under these circumstances, I found it difficult to be hopeful, but what other choice did I have? Her arms and legs were swollen. The nurses told me that her perineum (private area) was red and swollen, and it must be painful. She had sores in her mouth due to a fungal infection, but she did not complain much, to me anyway. I don't know if she was being so stoic to "protect" me. I, on the other hand knew, that she was uncomfortable, but more importantly, I was worried which of these myriad complications could be the fatal one. As a physician, I have seen and taken care of many seriously ill people, several of whom have passed away, but this was a completely different experience. Friends and colleagues try to be optimistic and encourage you, but no one can teach you how to cope with these circumstances. I felt very lonely, the person I had become used to leaning on for support, seemed to be slipping away from me.

On March 7, 1976, she appeared to be quite short of breath and Dr. Bowdler ordered a Venti mask (mask to give oxygen) at 5 liters /minute. This was a scary development for me because this event is frequently associated with people who are terminally ill.

On March 12, 1976, she appeared to be slightly improved. I ran into Dr. Campbell (One of her treating doctors, a hematologist) and he told me that the peripheral blood demonstrated exuberant phase of recovery with young granulocytes (white blood cells) forms. All features suggested either a complete remission or an effective partial remission. All I heard was the words complete or partial remission and I prayed silently for "complete remission". A bone marrow examination would have to be repeated to tell the whole story.

Although, she seemed to be improving during the last week, today she vomited blood. Dr. Campbell thought this was of esophageal origin. He also thought that she would not tolerate endoscopy (procedure by which one can look into the patient's esophagus and stomach). So, we asked for a gastrointestinal consultation. She was seen by another colleague (late, Dr. David Greenbaum). He put his hand on my shoulder and said ,"I am so sorry to hear this. I have been away (He had been away to Australia for a sabbatical) and had no idea what has been going on". Although I knew, he was sincere in expressing his sympathy, somehow it felt to me that this was the end. After all she had been through, and after a faint hope had developed in my mind that the bone marrow might be recovering, it looked like this GI bleeding (bleeding from her stomach) might be the terminal event. I tried to do my best to keep my composure. It was exactly midnight, and Dr. Greenbaum said he would scope her (look directly at her stomach with an instrument) to find out the cause of her GI bleeding. While he did that, I quietly retreated to the side room and despite my best efforts to the contrary, the tears simply kept rolling down.

March 16, 1976, she was transferred to ICU (Intensive care unit) indicating to me it was touch and go. A bone marrow aspiration was performed, and core biopsy (a small piece of bone is removed) was obtained without difficulty. Later in the day, we received a preliminary report, which stated "review of initial smears reveals a reduction of blasts to less than 5%. Megakaryocytes are abundant. Marrow appears to be in full remission".

I was ecstatic to hear this report and quickly went to tell her the results. My enthusiasm was obvious, but it was tempered by the fact that the GI bleeding was still ongoing. She said, "What good is the remission if the GI bleeding will not stop". I tried to tell her that with the remission, the platelets (blood cells that help in stopping the bleeding) number and function will improve, and most likely the GI bleeding will stop too. However, looking at the notes of Dr. Bowdler, who thought that the bleeding was due to erosive esophagitis due to Candida (fungus infection), I was not so sure of that myself. Her hemoglobin continued to drop and Dr. Bowdler ordered more blood transfusions.

March 18 1976, Dr. Greenbaum performed a gastric lavage (washing the stomach) again and more blood clots from the stomach were removed. He asked for a surgical consult and even before the surgeon could see her, I was thinking "no way is she going to tolerate any surgical procedures". She was, however, seen by a young surgeon (Dr James McGillcudy) who had just begun his practice after completing his fellowship. Instead of attempting any surgical procedures, he advised an epinephrine (a medicine that could stop the bleeding if instilled directly in the stomach) drip to be instilled directly into the esophagus. He assured me that he had tried this procedure during his training and in many instances, it resulted in stoppage of the bleeding.

The next 24-48 hours would tell if this procedure would work or would we have to resort to surgery. I was keeping my fingers crossed. As it turned out, the bleeding did slow down over the next 24 hours and appeared to have stopped over the next 48 hours. However, everyone was being especially careful. The doctors, although willing to discontinue the norepinephrine drip, were not yet willing to take the catheter (the tubing through which the medication was being instilled) out that was infusing the norepinephrine in case the bleeding started again.

On March 20, 1976, the progress notes indicated that "she was anxious to go home". I read that as a sign that she was indeed getting better; the bone marrow picture was compatible with a remission, and the bleeding, which appeared to be life threatening about 48 hours ago, seemed to have stopped. Coincidentally, I should mention, that exactly two days prior, her sister arrived from India. She brought with her from the temple of "SAI BABA" (a religious figure, who has been reported to perform miracles) small amount of ashes. I was told to apply that to her forehead, and she would be "cured". I obviously could not believe that the touch of ashes would perform the miracle. Nevertheless, I agreed to apply the ashes to her forehead, but refused to abandon the standard treatment that she was undergoing. According to the instructions from SAI BABA, all other treatments were to be stopped to allow the ashes to perform the miracle. Having said that, as I looked back at the events of the last two days, I couldn't help but wonder if the ashes did do some miracle after all.

March 24, 1976, she once again expressed a desire to go home, and Dr. Campbell said "we should discharge her home as soon as possible, husband and son's birthday on March,25"). But that was not to be. We talked about it, and I asked the nursing staff if I could bring my children to the hospital so our son could celebrate his birthday with his mother, even though it was going to be in the hospital. They were more than agreeable. So, I planned to be there with the children the next day to celebrate our son's birthday.

The day of his birthday, all four of us were in her hospital room, and for the first time in about two months there was a smile on my wife's face. Obviously, she was happy to see her children and participated in the celebration. I was cautiously optimistic. I was hoping that the "remission" would be a permanent or at least a long lasting one, but I was afraid it may or may not be. Nevertheless, the only hope, and therefore the only course of action we had, was to hope for the best and proceed as if everything had returned to "normal" although the reality was that things were far from "normal".

Maneesh's birthday in the hospital (March 1976)

The next day (March 26) was uneventful, and finally on March 27/1976, almost exactly two months stay in the hospital, she was discharged from the hospital.

Dr. Bowdler wrote in the "order sheet" "Please thank all the nursing staff involved for an invaluable effort on behalf of this patient". I wish he had also written the following on behalf of the husband of this patient. The nursing staff had provided an invaluable service indeed. They of course, provided invaluable nursing service dealing with multiple complications because of her disease/treatment. They tended to her mouth when it was full of sores; they tended to her perineum (private parts) when it was inflamed. They applied creams and bandages to her ears when she developed blisters. They made sure that severe loss of skin in her elbow as a result of infiltrated IV and subsequent infection did not result in the loss of her arm. Although it was the physicians who ordered chemotherapy, blood transfusions, and multiple antibiotics to fight off the infections that ultimately brought the leukemia under control, it was the nursing staff that was responsible for keeping her physically as comfortable as possible, and it was because of them that my wife was coming home in one piece although weakened and fragile as she was.

As I brought her home through the garage, a friend, (Late Dr Narinder Sherma) who had been so helpful in multiple ways including taking care of the kids when I could not because I was running around between my job, hospital and other errands, had made and hung up a long banner "Welcome Home!" I was pleased that she was finally home, but as I looked at her, she was so fragile. Only two months ago, she was a picture of health, and today she looked so thin and fragile. She must have lost about 20 pounds of weight and that could mean about 20% of her body weight. Her complexion, which used to be "fair" now appeared dark. The beautiful hair that she had, had been lost as a result of chemotherapy, and she was now wearing a wig. However, none of these physical changes mattered. I was delighted to have my wife back home and the kids were delighted that mommy was home even though she was too weak to do much for them.

Things gradually began to appear to be moving towards "normal". However, I do not think that the life of people who have survived a cancer can ever return to "normal". Even though all of us are aware of our own mortality, the feeling of mortality remains in the background, but for those of who have survived a cancer, the mortality remains in the forefront. The monthly injections of her chemotherapy were a constant reminder that we needed these injections to keep the leukemia at bay. Although still quite weak, fortunately she was able to take care of the activities of daily living. All that did not matter, because we were immensely thankful to have her back home, and I found myself silently praying that even if she does not do anything in and around the house, but simply be able to sit in a chair and be around the kids, would be more than anything else I could ask for.

Dr. Elisabeth Kubler Ross and David Kessler had described 5 stages of grief. (27) These include denial, anger, depression, bargaining and finally acceptance. We had already gone through the stages of denial, anger, depression, and we were (at least I was) in the stage of bargaining, ready to make a "deal" with the Almighty to spare her life.

A few days after Veena was home, her mother traveled from India to be with us. She would not only be able to take over some of the household chores while the kids went to school, and I went to work; she would be a constant source of strength for both of us, particularly her. As mentioned above, we had moved into this newly built house only a few months previous. The house was nowhere near furnished, but the furniture was on order. One day out of the clear blue sky, she said to me "Why don't you cancel the order of the furniture". I won't be around to see, use or enjoy the furniture. Those words "stunned" me, and I was left speechless. For a moment, I also thought that perhaps she was right. In addition, from my selfish point of view, what was I going to do with the furniture if she was not around. I probably would not be living in this house without her anyway. However, in the next moment, I thought to myself and said to her "Why do you say that?

You are now in full remission and hopefully the remission will last forever".

She: But what if it does not!

Me: Honey! There are no guarantees in life or of the life itself. Who is to say, how long am I going to live?

She: But you are well and healthy, and I wish you a long life. On the other hand, it seems to me that I am living on borrowed time, which could be very short.

Me: But we cannot live in the constant fear of death. Let us look at this way. You are healthy now, and so am I, so why don't we make the best of the present time for now and for as long as we have it.

Needless to add that the furniture remained on order.

As the days passed, then the weeks passed, she was getting her strength back. We began to enjoy the summer and would frequently sit on the deck to enjoy the long sunny summer days. The backyard of our house was devoid of any flowers because none had been planted, but the tall green trees and the newly established lawn provided enough greenery to provide a serene, soothing, and relaxing environment. I found myself thinking silently, "Enjoy these moments because who knows how many more of these we may have". However, a few days in the summer of Michigan can get very hot, and our house had no air conditioning. After the first real hot day, I said to her "We need to have an air conditioner installed", to which she responded once again "Why do you want to spend all that extra money on this house", and once again I thought "No! Whatever number of days we have together, why not live-in comfort?" Fortunately, we could afford it, so the air conditioner was installed within the next few days.

These two incidents are but two examples of the state of our mind, and I suspect that of many survivors of cancers. Constantly looking up to a better future and yet not knowing what the future holds or for that matter, if there is going to be any future and so the life goes on as if one is on a teeter totter.

As Veena was getting healthier and stronger, her mother began to get anxious to return home. After all, she had left behind a husband and a son. She began to say, "Now she is well, and I should return home". I knew for sure that she had no idea that her daughter had been suffering from leukemia and that although she was in remission at this time, the remission could last for a very brief or a very long period. No one, including myself, had told her about the seriousness of the situation in keeping with the "Indian Ways", which were quite prevalent at that time. It was a common practice not to tell patients and some other family members if the patient was suffering from a serious illness like malignancy, based on the thinking that the patient and some family members like the mother and daughter in our case, may not be able to "survive" the news. So, one day, I decided that the right thing to do for me was to let her in on the "secret". I still remember my words "Mom! Veena has had 'blood cancer', and we have been able to control it. However, at the present time, her life is, as if she is walking on a big ball, which contains a bomb, a slight wrong move by her, or on its own, the bomb can explode any moment". Perhaps the description was too dramatic, but it adequately conveyed to her the seriousness of the situation along with the hope that the bomb may take a long time or perhaps may never explode. She understood that, became less anxious, and was willing to stay on with us for a little longer. I felt that her being here was also a source of strength for my wife, and we both wanted her to stay for as long as she could. Nevertheless, she could not stay with us forever, and after nearly 4 months of staying with us, she decided that it was time for her to return home. Another factor that determined the length of her stay in the US was that the US immigration authorities had only authorized her stay for 4 months. Although theoretically, it was possible to ask for an extension of her stay, it was generally considered to be quite difficult. The stance of the US Immigration was, and to some extent continues to be, that every applicant for a visitor visa is a potential immigrant and the US authorities discourage immigration of people to the US unless they belong to a special category, which has been declared to be in short supply. There are numerous examples of relaxation of rules from time to time, which were enacted to make it easier for physicians, nurses, physical therapists, and teachers to immigrate when these groups of professionals were thought to be in short supply.

It is strange how some dates leave an indelible mark on one's brain. I still remember the exact date that she left the Detroit airport for India, i.e., July 26, 1976. It was also exactly one day after the validity of her airline ticket expired. Our travel agent had to come up with some lame medical excuse and a penalty of $50 to get her the validity of her ticket extended by a day so she could travel. At that time, it appeared to be a small penalty to pay, because the tickets were not refundable and if she was unable to travel on that day, we would have to purchase a new ticket. Under the circumstances, a 50-dollar penalty was much preferred compared to 500 dollars the price of a new ticket.

It is interesting to take note of her observation that she related to her friends in India. For obvious reasons, due to the illness of my wife, she was not able to travel in the USA. All she could see was the Lansing area and whatever other interactions she had were with the immigration authorities. Perhaps in retrospect, the highlight of her trip to Lansing, was a trip to the Lake Lansing on a hot summer day, where she saw several young women dressed in bikinis and mini bikinis lying on the beach and soaking in the sun.

On her return to India, when people asked her about what she thought of USA, her answer was, "It is a strange country. Women are walking around practically naked, but nobody pays any attention". Coming from a country where women, young or old, do not even expose their legs, it is perhaps not surprising.

The other observation was that she found the immigration officers and the custom officers very impressive. She would say that those officers were extremely well dressed in their uniforms, and she found them highly responsible and even intimidating (There was no TSA in those days, and the security checks at the airports were nothing compared to today.) She would compare those with their counterparts in India, whom she did not find impressive at all. She would add that the "officers" in India looked more like peons rather than officers.

15

TRIP TO INDIA

As my wife began to get her strength back, life did seem to be returning towards "normal". She now had the energy to "play" with the kids and gradually, she began to take some of the responsibilities around the house. So, one day she says to me, "I would like to go to India." To which I responded, "What for?" For a moment, I thought she was suggesting that we move back to India, and I said to her, "You are not suggesting that we move back to India, are you?!" Going back to India at that stage of our life would not be a good idea at all. I was sure that if we had been in India at the time of the beginning of her illness, we would not have achieved a remission and would probably have lost her by now. It is not that the healthcare was not available in India or the doctors in India were any less knowledgeable or competent, but many of the medications used to induce a remission would not have been easily available. I felt strongly (and still do) that the physicians in India are every bit as competent as physicians anywhere in the world, and even if we could import all the medications needed, the care, particularly the nursing care would not have been the same. This is because the cleanliness, or lack thereof in the hospitals in India. The post chemotherapy infection rate would have been high, such that we could not have managed it. As it is, as mentioned above, the fever and infections, many of which remained undiagnosed, were a constant source of fear, such that, it appeared for many days in a row that even if the underlying leukemia came under control, would she be able to survive infections. Fortunately, I think it was the white blood cell transfusions, which were lifesaving during the process of induction of remission. White cell transfusion was a modality of treatment, which was not available in India at that time. This episode of her illness put an end to any thoughts that we might have had about returning to India for good.

Luckily, however, she was not suggesting that we move back, and responded, just so I can see my father and my siblings. Going to India for a visit appeared to be a welcome idea. After all, it had been almost 6 years since we were married and had left India to move to USA. During this time, we had been back only once and that was to celebrate the "Mundan" ceremony of our son. This is a ceremony during which the head of a son (and sometimes a daughter) is completed shaved.

It is interesting to note that the first hair cut is special, not only amongst Hindus but in most cultures throughout the world. It is often considered a rite of passage. In many western countries, it is seen as a milestone for the baby and is marked by saving a lock of child's hair. Details vary from sect, locality, family, and country. Although predominantly it is a religious ceremony, some scientific reasons for the benefits of Mundan have also been described (28). Some Native American tribes celebrate the first haircut with a ritualistic dance. In Kenya, among Masai and other tribes, young men have their heads shaved as part of initiation steps into manhood. Orthodox Jewish boys get their first haircut when they turn 3. In some African Caribbean communities, it is performed once the child begins to speak clearly.

Hindus perform this ceremony in the first or third year (odd years) of the child. They believe that the hair present in the womb may somehow represent "unhealthy" hair and may be associated with undesirable and haunting memories of previous lives (Hindus believe in reincarnation). Thus, the removal of this hair is supposed to protect the child from evil.

In one of Hindu scriptures (Yajurveda), one of the mantras means "Oh child, I perform this tuft ceremony so that you can obtain a long life, constructive power, strength and wealth, good progeny and vigor." In the old days, when infant mortality was very high, survival of the child to the age of one year was a happy occasion and called for a celebration.

As expected, our last visit to India was full of happy memories. Almost all my family members had got together, and we had a wonderful celebration around the Mundan Ceremony. However, the visit to India this time around had a different purpose, and the vibes around this visit were also quite different. Although not specifically stated, when she said that the purpose of this visit was to visit her father, siblings, and friends, I could not help but think that she must be contemplating that this may be her only chance to see them. (Unfortunately, that turned out to be true.) Medically speaking, I was not sure if it was "safe" for us to travel to India. Her immune system had been compromised and would remain compromised due to continued use of chemotherapy. Even today, and more so back then, when people traveled from USA to India, certain vaccinations were required. The question, however, was not which vaccinations would be required, but whether it was safe to give her any vaccinations and even if they were given, would they generate enough immune (protective) response to be effective. There were innumerable questions surrounding her health, which would either make it possible, or not, for us to travel. Nevertheless, when I approached her oncologist, to my pleasant surprise, he said that it was safe for us to travel to India, and he recommended no additional vaccinations because of the risk of vaccinations might be more than acquiring an illness if we were careful as we traveled through India. The timing of the visit was also critical. We could not travel during the months of July through September because of the monsoon season and abundance of mosquitos. We, therefore, planned to travel during the months of November through December, utilizing the Thanksgiving and Christmas holidays so that the children would not miss much of their school curriculum as well.

We had a good trip to India. My wife's brother had pledged that if she survived the acute episode of leukemia, he would travel to Vaishno Devi, the most sacred temple of India, according to Hindu mythology.

Accordingly, one of the highlights of our trip was to visit Vaishno Devi, accompanied by my wife's brother and his wife. The temple is located on the top of a hill at about 5200 feet above the sea level. To reach the temple, one must go up a mountainous terrain for a hike of 16 miles uphill. Today, there are helicopters that one can take to get to the temple, but in those days, the only way to reach the temple was to hike on foot or take a pony ride. Naturally, none of us wanted Veena to take the hike on foot so she used the pony ride intermittently. Incidentally, it is believed that to get the full "spiritual benefit", one needs to hike the distance as much as possible.

The overall trip to India was uneventful except one day she said to me "I have a sore throat." Naturally, I was scared because that is how her illness with Leukemia had started. I looked in her throat, and it appeared pretty benign, but we could not take any chances. I managed to get a blood count and a throat swab for culture, both of which were normal. I should mention that under normal circumstances, the blood count and throat swab culture would be considered redundant (not needed) lab tests, but I felt justified in getting those done because of the special condition of her health. Even though both these tests were suggestive of her throat problem being of a viral origin, I debated, if I should give her antibiotics anyway but decided against that. I got her some throat lozenges for symptomatic relief, and she got better over the next few days. To many lay people including my own family members, this much attention to someone who has an ordinary sore throat may appear to be excessive. As a matter of fact, one of my family members commented "He is being overzealous in taking care of her health." Little did they realize what I had gone through, and I was going to do everything I could to "protect" her from anything that may turn the tide for the worse.

Although the trip to India appeared uneventful as far as the health of my wife was concerned, it was not entirely uneventful for our family. During this trip, I lost my mother. During this trip, I had gone to visit my brother in a nearby town (Dehra Dun) while my wife stayed back with her aunt. On our way back, my brother and I took a bus to an intermediate stop (Saharanpur) from where we were to board a train to New Delhi. As it turned out when we reached Saharanpur, we found out that there had been a train accident, and all the trains arriving in Saharanpur were running several hours late. We had nearly 5 to 6 hours at least, to kill before our train was expected to arrive. There was nothing to do but wait. However, rather than waiting at the railway station, we decided to go into town and see a movie (an Indian movie of course). Many of the readers may not know that Indian movie business, now called Bollywood, produces the largest number of movies in the world.

Although I do not remember the name of the movie that we saw, I do remember that on our way back from the movie to the railway station, a black cat ran across our way. Although cats are loved pets in the USA, if a black cat crosses your path, it is considered a bad omen in India. As soon as that happened, my brother and I looked at each other but didn't say anything. Our expressions said everything there was to say. It was obvious to both of us what each of us was thinking, namely, something bad is going to happen, but we hoped that no such thing would happen.

We reached the railway station past midnight but there was no sign of the train. We were told that it could still be several hours before the train would arrive. It was clearly past midnight, and we were both tired. The "waiting room", a space provided by the railway authorities for the passengers to wait for their trains, was already overflowing with passengers who had been stuck at this place due to the accident with resulting delays in several trains. There was not even a place to stand in the waiting room, and there was no chance of finding a place to sit. Consequently, we returned to the platform, where one could at least stand. However, it was not long before the sleep was taking over, and we were left with no choice but to lie down on a blanket spread over the bare floor of the platform, which to say the least, was not clean at all.

As I laid down on the floor, I couldn't help but say to my brother, "Only a few nights ago, I was sleeping on a comfortable bed in an air-conditioned room of a Hilton Hotel in the USA and here we are today on a bare floor on a railway platform in India". He responded,

"Although, I am sorry to put you through this, I do admire your ability to adjust to a different set of circumstances". We must have fallen asleep because we were awakened by the noise of an arriving train. Finally, the train that we were supposed to take had arrived, and we boarded it, arriving at our destination (Ghaziabad) in the early hours of the morning instead of having arrived in the early hours of the evening before.

We took a rickshaw to go home from the railway station. We had not reached my brother's place when a neighbor of his stopped our rickshaw and said, "A terrible accident took place last night. Your mother got burnt last night and the extent of her burns was so large that we had to transfer her to a hospital in Delhi. She is currently admitted in the 'Burn Unit' at Safdarjung Hospital (a hospital of considerable repute)." The details of the accident were sketchy, and at that point, we were not interested in the details but wanted to get home and on to the hospital as soon as possible.

When we arrived at the hospital, our mother was asleep. She had been heavily sedated. I met with the attending physician, introduced myself as a physician, and he in turn assured me that he and the staff were doing their best in caring for her. But he was also candid in informing us that the prognosis was grave, one because of her age, (She was about 76 at that time) and secondly because of the extent of the burns. I informed him that since I had contacts in the USA, if there was anything that was needed but was not available in India, which may be available in the US, that I could arrange that. He assured me that he would, if such a situation did arise but did not expect it.

Over the next three days, I had the opportunity to observe the care of a loved one from the other side of the bed in India as well, having experienced that earlier with the care of my wife in USA. One of my cousins happened to be a member of the medical staff of the same hospital, and he was able to arrange for me to sleep at night in the "house staff on call room" so that I could be available at a moment's notice if need be. I was pleased that the care provided was excellent. The doctors taking care of her were competent, compassionate, and caring. The infrastructure, however, was less than desirable. There appeared to be shortage of nurses so that the doctor's orders were carried out in what appeared to be a long lag time or perhaps it was my anxiety which made it appear so. Unfortunately, the condition of my mother continued to go downhill. Although she was receiving lots of fluids, she was not able to maintain her blood pressure, which kept dropping to dangerously low levels. The doctors were giving her medications to improve her blood pressure, but they were not having any noticeable effects. Finally, she succumbed to her injuries in about 3 days. I was disappointed that during this time I was not able to communicate with her because all this time she was sedated and could not communicate. I was also disappointed by the very last act of the house officer, who was taking care of her, although I cannot find fault with his intentions. When my mother's heart finally stopped, they called it a "cardiac arrest", and he began the cardiopulmonary resuscitation (CPR). The bed in which she was laying down was sagging with each of the chest compressions, meaning that the chest compressions were not effective. After a few more compressions, I said to the house officer, "What are you trying to resuscitate? She is gone, and we should let her go peacefully. Even if you get her heart going, what will we have?" Painful as it was, I had to let her go. I still do not know where I got the courage in a few brief seconds to tell the house officer that it was time for her to go.

The next few days were spent in the rituals of the funeral, and finally it was time for us to return to the USA. As I was leaving for the New Delhi airport for our flight, I still remember thinking and praying to God, "you have taken the Senior Mrs. Gossain from us, will you spare the younger (junior) Mrs. Gossain?" Was I trading the life of my mother for the life of my wife? No! I had already lost my mother, and now I was begging Him to spare the mother of my children, but as we will see later, that was not to be!

We returned from India a few days before the beginning of the New Year (1977). Veena began to talk about resuming her residency. I suggested to her that she might consider returning to the residency as a part time resident. Although part time residencies are generally discouraged, fortunately in our town there was precedence for that. There were two young women who were doing residency in pediatrics on a 50% basis. Both were young mothers also. The two would complement each other and function together as one full time resident. Naturally, it would take them twice as much time to complete their residency. Thus, although there would be no problem starting a residency in a part time manner, and her program director was quite agreeable to let her start as a part time resident, she decided against it and instead wanted to resume her work on a full-time basis, saying, "I feel well. I think I can do the work that is needed, and I do not want to take twice as much time to complete my training." Thus, she began her residency again, and we began to feel that perhaps life was returning to "normal".

Our family (1977)

16

GETTING TENURE

While the personal struggle was going on at home, now for more than a year, my job and academic productivity continued as best as it could. Although I had been appointed in the "Tenure Track" at MSU, which I knew, but did not know what that meant. So, one day I asked my colleague and my boss (Dr David Rovner) what that meant. He went on to explain, "You have been appointed in the tenure track, on probation for 3 years. At the end of the 2nd year, we will let you know if you will be reappointed for an additional probationary period of 3 years. At the end of 6 years, you will either be promoted to the rank of Associate Professor with tenure, or your services will be terminated." As he was explaining this to me, I realized that the time for two-year evaluation was just around the corner. Although that was obviously an anxiety provoking time, I decided that even if they were to terminate me, I would still have a year to look for another job. So, I was not going to worry about that at this time. A few weeks later, I did receive information that my appointment had been renewed for another 3 years, which was a relief. Nevertheless, it was time to apply for promotion. Before coming to Michigan State University, I had been an Assistant Professor in the Division of Endocrinology at St. Louis University School of Medicine in St. Louis, Missouri. The chairman who recruited me had assured me that the time I had spent at St. Louis will be considered for promotion. So, I asked my immediate supervisor (Dr. Rovner) if I should apply for promotion. After evaluation of my accomplishments, he advised that I should, so I did. The application for promotion went through the usual administrative process from Department to College to University but was ultimately turned down at the University level. No particular "official" reason for the denial of promotion was provided. So, I returned to Dr. Rovner to find out why, and his response was, "I am the 'acting chair', and our dean is the 'acting dean', and I think there were not enough people fighting for you and that is why I think it did not go through, but not to worry, I am confident that it would go through next year". Disappointing though it was, I also felt somewhat relieved that it was not my credentials and accomplishments that were felt inadequate, but it was the process at that time, which had resulted in that outcome. It also brought to light, that promotion to the next level was not going to be easy, to say the least. Nowadays, applicants for promotion get detailed descriptions of reasons for denial if their promotion is being denied. They are also provided what they need to accomplish over the next year or two to assure that the promotion will get through next time around.

At about this time Veena did begin her residency on a full-time basis. Life seemed to be returning to near normal. Kids were in school (kindergarten and pre-kindergarten, and day care), and we were both busy with our careers. We both valued every day that went by as if it was a "gift" from mother nature and had to be cherished as best as we could. This continued until one evening in November (1977) when she came home and told me "I saw my own blood smears today, and I saw a few blast cells (Immature cells). I think my remission might be coming to an end." The news felt like a ton of bricks had fallen on my head, but I was quick to respond, "You are an inexperienced resident! What do you know! Did you talk to your attending?" She replied, "No, I did not want to bias him, but they would be looking at those slides anyway, and we will know." I said, "OK then! We will wait to hear from them finally. Until then, let us try and not worry about it."

However, it was easier said than done. That night was clearly a sleepless night for both of us, and the whole night was a déjà vu of the night about 2 years before, when the news of her diagnosis was first delivered to us. We did not say anything else to each other, but we both knew that none of us was sleeping, and we both knew what the other was thinking.

The next morning as I returned to work, my first stop was the office of Dr. Anthony Bowdler. I informed him what Veena had told me the evening before. He also did not want to believe that and said, "No! It is not likely because just a couple of weeks ago her blood count and everything was normal, but it is possible. I will go to the hospital and look at those studies myself, and of course, I will let you know." That evening, he did call me and informed me that yes, there were a few blast cells (immature cells, which would mean a recurrence), but he said that did not necessarily mean that it was a relapse. We will need to perform a bone marrow examination to determine what the situation was. Unfortunately, a few days later the bone marrow examination confirmed our worst fears, i.e., she had relapsed, and the disease was active again. "So, now what!" I asked Dr. Bowdler. He replied, "There is no need to panic. We will try another round of chemotherapy and hopefully induce a remission again. This is not the end Ved!"

Although I felt somewhat reassured, I also knew, that the chances of inducing a second remission were rather low. An appointment was made for her to be admitted to the hospital. We were to report to the hospital in the evening before so that the chemotherapy could begin early the next morning.

As we packed our bags to go to the hospital, we stopped at the entrance of our bedroom at the top of the stairs, and without saying a word, we hugged each other. It was a long, loving hug, which without saying a word conveyed everything. Before we knew it, tears were flowing down the eyes of both of us, as if we were saying to each other "I don't want to let you go". Finally! I said to her, let us have courage and hope and maybe we will beat it again. With those few words, we descended the steps holding each other's hands. The ride to the hospital was quiet. I had driven on those roads a thousand times before almost always to see other people who were ill, but this time it felt very different. Not a word was exchanged between the two of us until we reached the hospital. A bed had already been reserved for her, and the admitting clerk completed all the formalities. Soon we were on the 6th floor of the Ingham Medical Center. Over the years the hospital has undergone many name changes and is now known as McLaren Lansing. It was one of the medical floors, where I had served as an attending physician. As a result, most of the nursing staff knew me, and I felt reassured that there were several familiar faces. I felt relieved knowing that she would be well taken care of. I stayed with her for as long as I could but had to return home to be with the kids.

The chemotherapy began the next morning. It was a routine procedure for her doctors and nurses, and initially, nothing seemed out of the ordinary, but within a couple of days it began to show its toxic effects, namely nausea, vomiting, gradual loss of hair, which had regrown following the earlier round of chemotherapy. Once again, the white blood cells (cells that are needed to fight infection) became quite low, and she began to develop a fever. For her doctors, it was difficult to decide if the fever was because she might have acquired an infection or was it due to the drugs themselves that she was receiving. In any event, they decided to add antibiotics on the assumption that she had an infection although we did not know where and what kind of infection she might have. Most lay people do not understand that medicine is an in-exact science. They, almost always, think that their doctors know exactly what ails them and whatever medicine their doctors are prescribing them will cure their illness. However, that is not the case at all. Doctors, after listening to the history from the patient and completing a physical examination, arrive at some possible diagnostic options. They then order some laboratory tests, x-rays, or other tests to confirm or exclude the diagnostic possibilities. They then arrive at what they think is the most likely diagnosis. They are almost never 100% sure, but maybe there is 90-95% likelihood that they have arrived at the correct diagnosis. The same process applies to people under treatment when complications arise, such as fever or shortness of breath. Thus, I was well aware of the process and had practiced it myself on multiple occasions. However, now knowing that we were shooting in the dark, made me uncomfortable, but I had to accept the process because there are no better alternatives.

Unfortunately, as I am writing this, I don't have a copy of her medical records available from the Ingham Medical center. (The records became unavailable, 25 years after the discharge date. The description of her first admission above is as accurate as it can be because that has been retrieved from her medical records. So, the following details may be sketchy by dates, but I do remember salient events, which I will describe below). One might wonder why I did not write this story earlier. The simple answer is that it was too painful to write soon after her death. Over the years, I tried several times, but just could not bring myself to write it down, until finally when I "retired". I became more aware of my own mortality and felt that it had to be done now or it will never get done.

Over the course of the next several months, she had multiple admissions to the hospital for administration of chemotherapy and some for the complications of it. Each time, however, the progress appeared to be in the wrong direction. On one such occasion, as I went to see her in the evening, I noticed that her eyes were puffy and her face was swollen, but she was not aware of it and had not complained of any unusual symptoms. By the next day, however, the swelling had increased further, and her eyes were almost shut. As I went to see her again the next week, I was horrified. I knew she had developed "cavernous sinus thrombosis" (i.e., one of her major blood vessels in the brain had been blocked). This carries a very high risk of death. As I sat in her room, tears began to flow down my eyes. One of the nurses must have noticed that because she came up to me and said, "I am so sorry! I know what you must be going through. All I can tell you is that we nurses are doing everything we can to keep her comfortable, and she has the best doctors, who are doing everything that they can." I thanked her for her concern, regained my composure, prayed, and hoped for the best. As I left her room that evening to go back home, I made sure that I told her "I love you" (as I had told her on many occasions), no matter how she looked. Gradually and somewhat miraculously, the swelling of her face subsided (So, perhaps my diagnosis of cavernous sinus thrombosis was wrong after all, for which I was very thankful).

As the days and weeks passed, her disease continued to progress. It was obvious by now (March/April 1978) that remission was not a possibility. We began to think about and talk about alternative treatment options. One such possibility was a bone marrow transplant. Although bone marrow transplants these days are a routine procedure and have led to "cures" in many different types of cancers, bone marrow transplant had just begun in the 1970's and was still considered experimental. I approached her doctors to ask if we should consider the possibility of a bone marrow transplant as a treatment option. The first question Dr. Campbell, one of her treating doctors, asked me was, if she had an identical twin, the answer to which was -No. An identical twin would make it much easier for the bone marrow transplant to function if such an attempt was made. He then asked me how many siblings she had. Fortunately, she came from a large family and had three sisters and three brothers, who were alive and well, but they were all in India. One of her sisters also had died from a cancer at a young age, approximately the same age as my wife was at this time. We briefly discussed if their blood could be tested to see if one or more of them could be a bone marrow donor, but then Dr. Campbell went on to explain the procedure of bone marrow transplant. He reiterated that at this time the bone marrow transplant was an experimental procedure with a very low success rate. I think, he mentioned that only 5 to 10% of those procedures resulted in functioning bone marrow after the procedure. In addition, to prepare patients for the bone marrow transplant, patients were given whole body radiation. The whole-body radiation would kill the immune system of the recipient so that he/she could accept the transplanted bone marrow. He went on to say that many patients died due to overwhelming infections during this time while they were being prepared to receive the bone marrow. Clearly, it appeared that he was not enthusiastic about it, but I had to ask him "would you recommend that we attempt to get a bone marrow transplant", to which he replied, "I would not recommend it". The only place where bone marrow transplants were being done in those days was Seattle, Washington. I did get the name of the physician in charge of bone marrow transplant program and his contact information, thought about giving a call to him, but after discussion with Dr. Campbell, I never did call him. Instead, I decided that before I called him, I needed to talk to my wife as to how she felt about undergoing this procedure, which appeared to be quite difficult, fraught with serious complications with very little hope of success. After I explained the procedure to her in detail, she thought about it for a while and decided that she did not want to undergo the procedure after all. We never did inform our families back home in India that we had considered this procedure and decided against it. To this day, I am not sure if that was the right decision i.e., not getting a bone marrow transplant. When I see the current day success of bone marrow transplants, I can't help but wonder, "What if we had gone for it? What if that had been successful?" But obviously that was not meant to be.

We now began to talk about what was obvious to both of us, i.e., death and dying. One day I asked her if she would like to go back to India to be with her family to which she responded, "you and the children are my family". I asked her again if she would like to go visit her parents and siblings one last time. She also declined that saying, "I would not want them to see me in this shape". (By this time, she had become quite thin, weak, and clearly had the appearance of a very ill woman). I would want them to remember me the way I was when they saw me last time when I was well and healthy. I asked, "Do you want anyone of them to come to visit us here?" She said, "I don't know. Why burden them? Besides, what will they do here anyway! They may also feel worse seeing me in this shape."

However, I felt that the decision, whether her parents, one or more siblings, would want to come and see her in the waning days of her life should be left to them. I should add that travel from India was not so easy in those days. A visa was required for an Indian citizen to travel to USA (It still is a requirement), but in those days, to get a visa, the sponsor (in this case me) was required to submit an affidavit of support, certifying that the sponsor will be responsible for the support of the visitor including medical coverage so that the visitor will not become a liability of the US government. To prove that the sponsor had the ability to provide such a support, the documents required to be submitted to the US embassy in India included:

- A letter from the employer including a statement of the annual income and whether the job was temporary or permanent.
- Residential address indicating if this was a rental/owned property.
- A statement from the sponsor's bank indicating that there was at least a $10,000 balance.

Fortunately, it was not difficult for me to arrange for these documents and so I sent a letter of sponsorship to her parents, asking if the parents or any of the siblings wanted to come to USA, explaining they were more than welcome and that these documents should be able to get them a visa to travel to USA, Painful as it was, in the accompanying letter, I had to indicate that she was now terminally ill, and this may be their last opportunity to see her if they so desired. However, none of them opted to travel for reasons best known to themselves. To this day, I have not had the courage to ask any one of them what led to this decision.

Then one evening while she was resting in bed, and I was sitting in a chair next to her, she asked me, "What are you going to do when I am gone?" I answered, "I don't know". She said, "I think you should get remarried." I said, "No!" She said, "It will be difficult to go through life without a partner. You will need someone to take care of you and the children. They are quite small." I said, "OK! If I get remarried, I can get a wife, but where will the kids get their mother? And who knows how my new wife will treat our kids?" She said, "It is possible that you will meet a young lady, who would not only be a good wife, but also a good mother to the kids." I said, "I don't know. We will see!" We left it at that because neither one of us wanted to go on with any further details of this topic.

While all this was going on, my job and my academic career was not on hold, although I wished it was. I remember trying to make a deal with the Almighty that if He would spare her life and even if she could do nothing but sit in a chair all day, I would not ask for anything else in life. But such prayers are seldom answered. So, I had to continue to do the best I could with my job. I must also add that people at work were very supportive and that was very helpful to me.

It was time once again to apply for promotion. There were times when I thought, why bother, because nothing else except the health of my wife mattered at that time, but then I would say to myself, "whatever is happening to her is not in my control" and life must go on. Therefore, I needed to do things that were required including applying for promotion. I applied and forgot about it until late in the month of June when I was informed that the promotion was not approved. But this time we had a new (and permanent) chair (Dr Raymond Murray). So naturally, my first response was to go and ask him as to why the promotion was denied. His response, although somewhat accurate, surprised me. He stated that the Department's Promotion and Tenure (P and T) committee had recommended a promotion, and he had strongly endorsed it. He went on to say that he had even mentioned in his supporting letter that I was a "minority" faculty. By saying so, he was indicating to me that since I was a minority faculty, this made the case for my promotion even stronger. When he mentioned that, it dawned on me as to why I was on all the Department and several College level committees even though I was a junior faculty. I was the token "minority" faculty representative on all those committees. As I look back, I was the only "minority faculty" in the department at that time. This is how the institutions comply with the laws of equal opportunity and demonstrate that minorities are not discriminated against. Whether the presence of a minority faculty on various committees actually prevents discrimination is another matter.

In any event, he advised me that I should go and see the dean and ask him as to why my promotion was denied. Accordingly, I made an appointment to see him.

On the day of my appointment with the dean, I was slightly apprehensive. I had never been in the office of a dean. Even at the time of my recruitment and appointment, I had somehow missed meeting with the dean in his office. He may have been out of town or simply not available to meet with a junior faculty member prior to his appointment. As I walked into the dean's office, I was impressed by the size of the dean's office. The dean himself was a large man with a graying beard, and he looked like Santa Claus, sitting comfortably in an oversized chair. I explained to him the purpose of my visit, asking him as to why my promotion to the level of an Associate professor was denied despite a strong recommendation from the promotion and reappointment committee of the department and my chair? He responded by saying "I am going to make promotions difficult in the college. They have been too easy." I said, "I understand that completely, sir! But how difficult, and what are the criteria that one is supposed to meet prior to promotion?" To the best of my knowledge at that time, the college was still in its infancy, and the criteria for promotion were not well defined.

The dean said, "We evaluate your teaching ability, clinical care, competence and scholarly output before we can promote people." Luckily for me, just that morning I had received an evaluation from National Institute for Health (NIH) related to a grant application that I had submitted a few months ago. The research grant was approved (but not funded). As part of the evaluation of the grant application, the applicant (or principal investigator, in this case me) is also evaluated. The evaluator, whoever he/she was, was full of praise for me, stating that" Dr. Gossain was a promising investigator. He has very good credentials and has accomplished a lot during a short time".

I handed that letter to the dean and reminded him that prior to coming to Michigan State University, I was an Assistant Professor at St. Louis University School of Medicine for 2 years and at the time of recruitment, the chairman of the department of medicine had assured me in writing that the previous experience at St. Louis University will be considered for the promotion. I also handed that letter (which I still have in my possession) to the dean. The dean then fell back in his enormous chair, became more serious, and I became more nervous. He finally said "The promotion cycle is over, and it would be very difficult to change this decision this year. However, I am going to go back to the provost, and I will give you my word that I will do my best to get it reversed." It has never happened in the University before, but I will do my best". There was nothing more for me to do, so I thanked him and left his office. True to his word, he did get it reversed.

Meanwhile, the health of my wife continued to deteriorate. The aggressive chemotherapy intended to obtain a "cure" had been stopped, but the "supportive" treatment was continuing. The end was obvious and appeared imminent. At that time, there were not many Hindu Temples in and around the state of Michigan, or for that matter even in the USA. I began to wonder if there were any priests or practitioners of Hindu religion who might be available to perform the last rites. The nearest and only Hindu Temple I could find was one lead by ISKON (International Society of Krishna Consciousness) in Detroit. This society had been founded by a learned and knowledgeable expert of Hindu religion (Sri Prabhupad). He had founded this society to spread the Hindu religion in the West and most of the followers were local white people. Many of the immigrant Hindus also became his followers because there were no other "traditional" Hindu temples at that time. Hinduism is an ancient religion and has many variations of how this religion is practiced around the world. Finally, I was able to contact a priest by phone at the ISKON temple and asked him if there were any individuals who would be able to perform the last rites when my wife expired. My sister-in-law (Geeta, Veena's sister) who was standing nearby broke down as soon as she heard the word last rites and cremation. Obviously, crying, she ran upstairs to be alone in her room. I was relieved that there would be someone available when the final moment arrived. He also advised me to check with local funeral homes to see if cremation facilities were available in the Lansing area, which I did and was relieved to find out that, there was at least one cremation facility in our area, quite nearby.

Then one day, Veena called me while she was in the bathroom because she could not get up from the toilet seat (She did not have the strength to get up.). I helped her get up and noticed that the toilet bowl was full of bright red blood. She did not have a bowel movement but had passed a large amount of blood. No wonder she did not have the strength to get up. As she got up, I noticed that her clothes were also soiled. I must have felt annoyed and said to her "couldn't you just wait a minute"? However, as soon as I said that I realized how stupid of me to ask that question. If she could, she would have waited. I felt guilty and remorseful. I helped her change into clean clothes, took her to bed, and to make sure that she was ok, I checked her pulse and blood pressure. As expected, the blood pressure was a little low and pulse slightly rapid but not dangerously so. There was no need to panic or call an ambulance. So, I decided to wait it out, hoping that no further bleeding would occur. That night as we were ready to fall asleep, I said to her "Veena! Brief as it has been, we have had a good life together, but the last few months have been particularly difficult. I have tried my best to be helpful and supportive, but if I have failed you anywhere along the way, please forgive me". Without any hesitation, she responded "No! You have been a good husband. I could not have asked for anyone better." I don't recall if those were her last words to me, but those are the last words that I remember, and they have been a cherished memory that I still carry with me, and strange though it may seem, were a source of strength for a long time even after she passed away.

It was not long after the above episode that one morning as we woke up, I called her name, wanting to ask her how she was feeling, and if I could get something for her. She did not respond, even after I tried a few more times. I checked her pulse, blood pressure, breathing and temperature. Everything was functioning normally, but she was simply unresponsive. I was concerned so, I called her doctor (Dr. Anthony Bowdler), who said that he would come over to the house and look at her. He came and examined her in his usual thorough way and with a serious and somber voice said "Ved! I think she is dying." We can take her to the hospital, give her some fluids intravenously (IV), and possibly antibiotics, and she would improve, but the improvement will only be temporary and will really amount to prolonging her misery. I suggest that we do nothing at this time. She is comfortable and peaceful. I know it is hard but let us have her go peacefully". Even though it was expected, I was stunned to hear those words from Dr. Bowdler. I was speechless for a few minutes.

Once I regained my composure, I said to him, "Ok! We will do as you say!" But let me add, that although that decision was made over a few minutes time, that was the hardest decision of my lifetime, and I wish and pray that I will never have to decide anywhere near close to that situation in my remaining lifetime. I got hold of "Bhagwad Gita", a holy Indian spiritual book and started to read to her. The legend has it that if you prayed by the side of a dying person or read a holy book, he/she will go to heaven. My thinking was that not only I had wanted her to have the best in this world, but I also wanted the best for her in the next world. I did derive some strength from some of the words in the holy book such as "The soul is indestructible, the swords (or weapons) cannot destroy it, fire cannot burn, and water cannot destroy it." Just like we get rid of old clothes and put on newer clothes, similarly the soul leaves the present body and is reincarnated into another until it achieves "Nirvana" and escapes the cycle of life and death. (Hindus believe in reincarnation and Nirvana).

There was nothing else to do or say. She was non-communicative at that time. All I remember is, that I kept reading that holy book all day in a voice loud enough so she could hear me. I was hoping that although she could not speak, she could hear me, and these spiritual words would do her some good in her next life. I don't even remember where the kids were. It was the month of August, so there was no school. My cousin's wife from Houston (Sita Gosain) had graciously come to stay with us. She was taking care of her kids as well as ours. The kids were probably busy playing with their cousins, enjoying the nice outdoors that we get in Michigan in the summer months, oblivious to the fact that what was happening in the bedroom upstairs was about to change their lives forever.

It was about 8 pm on August 15, 1978 that she finally breathed her last breath. I was too stunned at that time to react emotionally in anyway, and I kept on operating mechanically. I remember, there were no more tears in my eyes, perhaps I had cried enough during the last several weeks or months.

Almost as soon as she was gone, I went to the telephone and called the funeral home to let them know what had happened. They said that they would be over in a few minutes to take the body to the funeral home. As soon as they arrived, their first question was if she had been under the care of a doctor and whether I would be able to get them a "death certificate", which I assured them that I would. It seemed very intrusive and almost offensive for them to ask questions like these, when someone has just lost a loved one, but the law does not stop at the time of death. It almost seems like that there are more legal formalities that need to be completed in the case of death than in the case of living beings.

As the funeral home people prepared to take her away, I remember kissing her and saying "Goodbye! My love." Then I went down and brought the kids back up so they could take one last look at their mother and said to both of them "Beta! (Child) Mom is going away forever".

I don't know what they might have been thinking at that time. They were aged 6 and 5 years respectively. At that time, I think they were old enough to realize that people who die do not come back but young enough not to realize what the consequences of the death would be on their lives. I don't recall them crying or expressing any other emotions at that time.

The next couple of days are a complete blur in my mind. I mechanically kept on taking care of the arrangements for cremation and funeral. My cousin, Narendra Gossain, who had been more than a brother to me in this country flew in from Houston. I went to pick him up at the airport and when I met him, I cried like a child on his shoulder. I don't even know how the word got around, but there were so many people at the funeral home. My friends going back to my medical school days from all over USA, colleagues from work, her colleagues from her place of work, neighbors, parents of our children's friends, everybody I knew were all there. The priest also arrived from the ISKON temple as planned. After a few introductory remarks and a couple of mantras, he poured some "ganga Jal "(Water from the river Ganges in India) in her mouth. it is believed that if the holy water from the river Ganges is poured in the mouth of the deceased person, he/she will then proceed to live in the heavens. He then began to chant "Hare Rama, Hare Krishna, Krishna, Krishna, Hare, Hare". Pretty soon the entire audience was chanting the above Bhajan (Religious song), the whole funeral home auditorium appeared to have changed into an auditorium of any Hindu temple. After the service was over, the priest commented to me that he had never seen so many Americans participating in a Hindu service and reciting the Bhajan (religious song) with such sincerity as if this was one of their own. This may have been the best compliment or farewell that the departed soul could have received from her local community in which she had barely lived for only about 3 years.

The service was then followed by everyone leaving for the cremation grounds where her body would be cremated. An important question at this juncture was whether the kids should accompany us to the cremation or not. One of my aunts (my mother's sister) happened to be here and I turned to her for advice. She and some friends also advised that the children were too small to understand what was going on and the experience may be too traumatic for them.

It is generally believed that children under the age of 7 are too young to understand the meaning of death and should not attend funerals. Some authorities recommend that after the age of 7 a child may attend a funeral if he or she wants to. However, it is difficult to assess at the time of death if a child really understands and can make such a decision. According to one British social attitude survey nearly half the individuals (48%) still think that it is inappropriate for children under the age of 12 to attend funerals (29).

As a result, our children did not accompany their mother to her last journey and were left behind with some friends, who graciously agreed to take care of them at this difficult hour of my life.

17
THE ACCULTURATION CONTINUES

As far as the process of acculturation of immigrants is concerned, we were still in the "state of struggle". The stage of struggle lasts for a variable period, depending on the individual circumstances. In our case, the struggle to survive in the professional world had been complicated by the struggle to survive in a literal sense at home and we had lost that battle as far as my wife was concerned. The struggle for me and the children, only became much more difficult, because a critical person of the team was now missing.

Following the funeral, I decided to go to India for a few days to meet the rest of my family and hers in India. It is said that if you share your grief, it gets reduced, and if you share happiness with people that care for you (or you care about), the happiness gets multiplied. It was perhaps for my own sanity that I needed to get away from East Lansing and the best place I could think of was to retreat to India to be with my family. I had no plans as to how long I was going to be away and what I was going to do while I was there. It was right around that time that our chairman (late Dr. Raymond H. Murray) who was vacationing in Charlevoix, Michigan called me from his boat and said, "I am very sorry to hear about the passing of Veena, and I understand that you are going to India. Go to India, take as much time as you want or need. Do not worry about anything over here. We will take care of it."

I cannot even describe how supportive and helpful those few words were. I have not forgotten them to this day and every chance I get to talk about Ray Murray, I relate this little story to whoever will listen.

However, at this time, my grieving had just started. Before I left Detroit for New Delhi, I called my older brother who had been a father figure to me since the death of my father while I was still in the medical school (1963) and told him about the details of my flight. He in turn promised to meet me at the Palam Airport (now called Indira Gandhi airport). He, being a railway officer, took the train from Madras (now called by its original name Chennai) to Delhi while I took the flight from Detroit. As it turns out, I reached Delhi a few hours before he did. I relate this little incident only to indicate that first generation immigrants from India, including me, often think that we are too far away from home. But this incident only confirms that although we may be far away distance wise, the time to travel back to India may not be that long. In any event, I did go to India, and it was a relief to meet with the near and dear ones and share my grief with them. The load did appear to lighten up quite a bit. There was again, one more religious function of her last rites and once again, a large crowd had gathered to pay their respects to her. The final act was to put her last remains, (ashes) which I had carried with me from the US into the holy river Ganga. For that I traveled to Haridwar, a holy city about 300 Kilometers from Delhi accompanied by my brother. (The word Ganges has been used to represent this river by the British when they ruled India.) It is believed by Hindus that putting the last remains (ashes) into the river Ganga leads to the peace of the departed soul and perhaps "Nirvana", i.e., freedom from the cycle of life and death forever. The site where these rituals are performed is extremely crowded. Not only the families of the deceased are gathered here, but there are many pilgrims, and many "priests" are available to perform the last rites. Many of these priests are designated priests for individual families. The families of these priests have served many generations of these families. Looking at the crowds, it does not seem possible that the priest of your family will find you, but miraculously they do, at least the priest of our family did find us. After the last rites were performed, he took us to his cabin and opened his book to show us the entries made by my family members such as that when my father brought the ashes of his mother (my grandmother) in 1942, my grandfather in 1946. The entries included the date, the names of the family members and the signatures of those who had visited him. Needless to add, that we were able to identify the signatures of our family members and were quite sure that the entries were authentic. Their books not only contained entries about the sad events, but also about the happy events of the family, such as "Mundan ceremony" of my nephews for which I was physically present had been accurately recorded. In these days of computers, it is truly amazing how these simple people, who are not highly educated except in their ability to perform religious ceremonies, are able to keep accurate records of the generations of families. I asked the priest if I could make copies of the relevant pages, which he promptly refused, arguing that it is how they make their living. After they show you these entries made by your family members, they expect a hefty "Dakshina" (Dakshina is a tip that is given out of gratitude) which we did and left his cabin for the return journey to Delhi.

One chapter of my life had thus closed and a new one was about to begin. No matter what happens, life must go on. It was time for me to decide how my life was going to progress from here on. According to the stages of acculturation described by Majumdar, by now, I should have been entering the "Stage of Anxiety". However, my "Stage of Struggle" had been complicated by the personal struggle that we had been through. Friends and relatives were forthcoming with their advice as to how I should go on. Most of them were advising that I should return to India for good. The luck (good or bad) had given me another opportunity to evaluate if our life (mine and the children) would be better in the USA or in India.

Most of all, I valued the advice of my older brother (Lajpat Rai) who, as I mentioned earlier, had been a father figure for me during the last many years since my father had passed away in January 1963, while I was still in the medical school, and he was almost 20 years my senior. By this time, he had reached the peak of his professional career.

He was a career government officer in the Indian Railways and had achieved the rank of "General Manager", which I believe is the highest rank that he could have achieved. He was the chief of the "Integral Coach Factory" located in the south of India near Chennai. In terms of hierarchy among government officers, he commanded authority just below the governor of the state of Tamil Nadu (The state where he was located). He was quite insistent that I should not only settle down in India, but in fact locate in the same town where he was living. He said to me, "In a few months, I am going to retire from the government service, and I will settle down here in this town itself. We have lots of friends in this town, and they would be very helpful if we need their help. You should come to Chennai and see for yourself how good the town is and whether you would like to live there."

So, we did go to visit him. It was a nice cosmopolitan city located on the ocean. He was living in a mansion provided to him by the government. It used to be the governor's residence during the British Raj. He was also making the case that if I decided to stay back in India, finding household help would not be a problem and would be easily affordable, compared to USA. To make sure that I would have no trouble settling into my profession of medicine and Endocrinology, he introduced me to the chief medical officer of Indian Railways, who was very encouraging, and he was quite sure that if I would start a private practice of Endocrinology, I would be very busy in no time. He knew that diabetes was quite common in India including the state of Tamil Nadu. He was so confident because at that time (1978) Endocrinology was not a well-developed specialty in India and the people in that metropolis were educated enough to realize the need and were affluent enough to willingly pay for such services. At that time, the concept of health insurance had not yet developed in India. To make sure that I could explore other options, such as being an employed physician, he also introduced me to a Dr. Reddy, who was the founder of the Apollo Hospitals. At that time, he had just established one hospital, but in the last 40 years or so, it has matured into a large chain of for-profit hospitals, and they are now doing a flourishing business all over India and even outside of India. Dr.

Reddy must have been impressed by me and my credentials, such that he offered me a job on the spot, which included a guaranteed salary and opportunity to have a private practice on the side. I must admit that the offer was tempting such that I was seriously considering it.

That evening, however, my daughter began to complain, "Dad! I do not feel good." As I touched her hand, it was obvious that she was running a fever. I thought to myself, she must have caught a virus or something similar and she would be fine in a few hours or a day or two. However, in a couple of hours, her body was burning and when we checked her temperature, it was 104° F, and she was becoming drowsy. Now I began to think of some serious viral infections of the central nervous system, although I knew that the fever itself could be making her drowsy. Doctors almost always think of the worse possibilities when it comes to their own health or that of their immediate families and our case was no exception. In any event, I began to put cold compresses on her forehead and gave her some Tylenol. Fortunately, in a few hours, her fever settled down and by the morning, she was feeling much better. During the hours that she was febrile, I could see clearly, a look of great anxiety and concern on the face of my brother and his wife. Once the fever settled down, he expressed to me "Thank God! You were here. I don't know what we would have done without you, and this sick child on our hands". One of the options that we were considering was that I could leave the children in the care of my brother and sister-in-law, and I could return to the USA. That option clearly became untenable because it was obvious that they would not feel comfortable taking care of my children when I was 10,000 miles away.

The following evening, we just went out to see the city, and my brother stopped at a gas station to get some gas for the car. It became interesting to see that he could not communicate with the gas station attendant. He was telling the gas station attendant to fill the gas, check the oil and the tire pressure, but the attendant was acting like he did not understand a word. He only spoke and understood Tamil, while my brother could speak Hindi, Punjabi, and English, but no Tamil. Finally! The manager of the gas station came out of his office. He spoke and understood English, and the job was done. India has many different languages and dialects. Situations like this are common, where two people from the same country can only communicate with each other only in English or not be able to communicate at all. I must admit that I thought to myself that if I were to settle down in this town, situations like the one we had just experienced would be common, and I would feel more "foreigner" in my own country as compared to how I felt in the USA. Consequently, it cemented the idea in my head that this was not the place I wanted to settle down in. Moreover, as it turned out, my brother, after his retirement, also did not stay in that town any way. After retirement from the government service, he was offered a lucrative position in the northern part of India, where he felt more at home, and he had a job that he enjoyed for a few more years. In retrospect, that decision appears to have been the right one.

We stayed with him for a few more days. It was relaxing, free from the worries of job, but constantly thinking, what next?! Then one day he said that he was traveling to another city about 300 miles away on an "official business", and we could accompany him if we wanted to. Since we had nothing better to do, we readily agreed. As we entered the railway coach that we were to travel in, I was amazed to see that it was a whole house on wheels. It had a living room, couple of bedrooms, and a fully equipped kitchen. There was staff to prepare meals and cater to any needs that we might have. It was truly a luxurious train, something that I had never experienced before and neither had my children. A few days before our trip, he had travelled in the same train with the prime minister of Ireland, who was on an "official" visit to India and this railway factory in India to purchase some railway carriages for the Ireland railways. We had a very enjoyable and the most comfortable railway journey better than the one we ever had before. So, it was no surprise that when people asked my 5-year-old son "What did you like about India?" he would say "I liked my Uncle's train". To this day, he tells me, "That is the way to travel, Dad!"

By this time, it was middle of September 1978, and it had been almost a month that we had been in India. The children's school in the US had been open now for a couple of weeks, and if we were to return to USA, now was the time to do so, since they were already missing school. Although, I had no definite date that I had given to MSU for my return, it was time to do so. While I was still toying with my options, I was up and down, i.e., stay in India for good or not, return to USA or not, a telegram was received from my Department, "After so much bad! A little bit of good! Your promotion was approved. Ray Murray." The promotion also meant that I would be now a "tenured" professor. As if this was the last piece of the puzzle that I was looking for, I decided that it was time to return to USA. We will see how it goes, and if there is reason to return to India, that can be done at any time. One of my sisters-in-law (brother's wife) agreed to accompany us to East Lansing to initially help with the children until we could make some more permanent arrangements. For that, I am eternally thankful to her and once again, it restored my faith in the family. These days most of the family units including my own have shrunk down to nuclear family units and by and large they have no idea how helpful members of the extended (or joint) family can be in times of need.

A few days after my return, the Department administrator handed me a slip (ironically, I think it was a pink slip) confirming my promotion and the granting of tenure. When I asked him what did the tenure mean? He said, you now have a permanent job with MSU for life. You have the academic freedom to pursue whatever you like, and if you ever have a major disagreement with your chair, you don't have to give in (Although that is what I was told, I would discover later that it is not entirely true).

I asked the same question of Dr. Rovner, and he responded "when I got tenure at University of Michigan (U of M), I went to the human resources department of U of M and asked them what tenure means, and they said "Professor Rovner! We will always call you Professor Rovner" Implying that there was no job security, but apparently at MSU, this provided for some job security and academic freedom although as we shall find out later, both the job security and academic freedom are only to a limited extent.

After the return to US, the world around me behaved as if nothing had changed. However, my life was anything but like what it had been before the catastrophic event. The day after our return, I accompanied my children to their elementary school (Pinecrest of East Lansing). I had to go to the main office to find out which class they had to go to, even though the school had been open for almost three weeks. As I took one child at a time to their respective class, I introduced myself and my child to their teacher. I felt that I had to tell the teachers that this child has just lost his/her mother so please treat them with extra love and care. As I uttered those words, it was hard to keep my composure, and I ended up saying to the teachers "I am sorry! Men are not supposed to cry, but I could not help it!" The teachers were of course very understanding and assured me that they indeed will provide extra care to the children, and the fact that they had missed the school for a few weeks was of no consequence because we could make that up, because after all, they were only in kindergarten and first grade.

Although, my sister-in-law (my brother's wife) had accompanied me to the US to help me with the transition of making more stable arrangements for the kids, we decided that the kids should continue to go to an after-school program at a "day care center", where they would have friends with whom they could interact and play with, rather than come home to an empty house and "miss" their mother even more. It only meant that I had to make arrangements of carpooling with some other parents so that we could pick the children up from the day care centers at appropriate times. This would mean that sometimes I would have to decline to attend a meeting after regular hours, and I would also need to make sure that when it was my turn to pick up the children that I was not in the clinic just in case the clinic ran late. This led to the realization of the problems that only single parents have to face. Almost simultaneously I discovered that there existed a club called "single parents of East Lansing". One of the single parents from this group invited me to join the club. The members of this group were single parents, either through the death of the spouse or more often through divorce. Thus, although certainly single, I did not find much in common with the members of this group. The group met about once a month, usually in a bar and talked about common problems of the single parents over a few drinks. Sharing common problems and looking for solutions among people in the same predicament was certainly helpful. Members of the group were also willing to pitch in to help each other in case of need. However, it did not take long for me to discover that one of the hidden agendas was to look for a prospective partner from among the members of the group itself. I was not particularly interested in this aspect of the group. The group also planned some activities on weekends or in the evenings to which either I could not go or did not find interesting enough to want to go to. The latter began to make me think that perhaps I did not "fit" in with the crowd, which made me paranoid to some extent. By this time, I had been in the USA for almost 11-12 years. So why did I not fit in with this group, with which at least superficially, I had a few things in common? Some introspection and some discussion among friends made it clear that it was not an uncommon phenomenon among the first generation of immigrants. It is at that time that I discovered that immigrants from different countries had been congregating with people of similar background. They not only socialized with people of similar background, but also tended to live in same neighborhoods. That is how localities like "Little Italy", or "little Havana" had come into existence. So, one day I asked a colleague who was originally from England, how well he had assimilated in this country. He responded that "it was difficult to fit in, in this society". His response clearly surprised me, because I had thought that he was from the "old country" and his assimilation would have been much easier than mine based on our widely different backgrounds. This realization was actually a relief in that what I was experiencing was nothing out of the ordinary, and I was not going to be the first one to break this cultural/social barrier.

When one loses a spouse that one had loved dearly, the first reaction is "I do not want to live without her". However, that reaction, although very strong emotionally, does not get converted into a reality. Most people go through a period of "grieving" for a variable period but do find a reason to go on with life, although occasionally the living spouse may go through a period of real "depression". It is a common observation among older couples who have been together for a long time that frequently after the death of one of the partners, the other will pass away within a year or so. In my case, the obvious reason to live was my children. They had just lost their mother and now it was my responsibility to give them the love and affection of both their mother and father. It appeared to be a daunting task, but I had no idea how hard that was going to be. Then one day, one of the colleagues in the department (Dr. Andrew Michelakis), who also had lost his wife to death a few months before I lost mine, sat down with me and tried to assure me that hard as it was, I will be able to get through this and life will go on. He went on to relate that in the absence of his wife, he had to explain the facts of life to his young daughter, who had just entered puberty which he found hard to do but was able to get through it. The immediate cause of concern was to make some arrangements for an adult to be with the kids after school when I had to be at work. It was around that time that I became a strong believer in the theory that when God puts you in an adverse situation, He/She also gives you the strength to cope with it and the solutions emerge to manage the situation. One such example is my own case and that is, the spouse of another colleague in the department (Mary Ann Bull), who was a social worker, invited me to her house and introduced me to a nurse (Sue Brennan). Sue was a registered nurse (RN), who worked full time but at night shift. She was willing to pick up the children from school at about 3 pm, although most of the time they walked back home by themselves, cook dinner, eat dinner with us and stay with the children until she had to go to work at 11 pm. She was happy to do it for what appeared to be rather small financial compensation because she wanted to and was glad to help for the sake of children. Under the circumstances, what else could I ask for? She was a nurse and would of course be helpful in case the kids were sick or hurt themselves, and she could be there for several hours after the school ended. We both readily agreed on this arrangement. As soon as this was finalized, my sister-in-law, who was living with us for the last couple of months, began to make plans to return to her family in India. She had been getting anxious to return to India and be with her husband, rather than stay in the USA for any longer than necessary.

As mentioned earlier, the "Stage of Struggle" then transitions into a "Stage of Anxiety". By now, at least theoretically, I should have been in the "Stage of Anxiety", but my "Stage of Struggle" had been prolonged due to the death of my spouse. Although, the "Stage of Struggle" appeared to have been completed from the professional side of my life, on the personal side, it was a different matter. Although, I had made arrangements for the kids to be cared for after school, it was obvious that it was only a temporary arrangement.

Then, one day on a weekend we went to the local "Art Festival" where there were a lot of vendors (Artists) selling their art. At one place, my daughter liked a necklace and we purchased it. The seller said to her "Are you buying this for your Mom? To which my daughter replied" I don't have my mom anymore, but I can give it to my aunt" (mom's sister)'. Although, she stated it almost like a matter of fact, watching her say this, my heart ached. I might have still been grieving, but it was apparent to me that the children needed a mother figure at home (contrary to what may be the modern thinking. I believed and still believe that in a stable home, there needs to be a father figure and a mother figure).

Once again, I was at a threshold, i.e., do I get married again, and if I do, how am I going to go about it, namely an arranged marriage once again or a love marriage? In either case, would my partner be a good mother to my children was the main concern. After quite a bit of soul searching, my Indian upbringing and Indian values prevailed, and I decided to find a partner through an "arranged" way. My family members back in India must have been thinking along the same lines. However, an arranged marriage is not like going to a grocery store and picking up a wife. It needs time and effort, and especially now in my case because there were children involved, the matter was even more complicated. I might add at this point that a widow or widower, especially with children, is considered a less than desirable match for young people who have never been married before. The school year was about to come to an end, and the children will be out of school from June until the beginning of September. I had no idea how the other single parents manage their children age 6 and 7 during the extended summer breaks. The only solution I could think of was to take an extended vacation and go to India. There, the children could attend school, stay with one of their uncles or aunts, and get to know their extended family in India. So, I asked for and was granted an extended vacation time. I got invited (or got myself invited) to be a visiting professor at All India Institute of Medical Sciences (AIIMS) in New Delhi. It was my Alma Mater and to return there as a visiting professor was both an honor and a privilege. When I approached my chair for his approval, to accept this position as a visiting professor at AIIMS, he responded," yes by all means. It is good for the International image of MSU". With this arrangement, while the children attended a new school in India I could also stay professionally connected. The schooling for the children, however, did not work out as planned, mainly because, although the children were young, they were used to "American" schools. I got them admitted to a "convent school", in Mumbai (Bombay) where the medium of instruction would be English, thinking that it would make the transition easier for them but that was not to be.

Within about a week, came one day when my daughter had not completed her "homework" assignment. When the teacher asked her where her homework was, she politely replied that she had not done her homework. The teacher went on to say that in that case, she must be punished so that in the future, she will not forget it again. As a punishment, she was asked to stand up on her chair so that the whole class would know that she was being punished for something. This was a common way of punishing children when I was in elementary school, and I guess that practice continues. My daughter, on the other hand, not being used to such practices, simply refused to do so and told her teacher "Ma'am! I am not going to stand up on my chair". I don't' know where a 7-year-old in a completely new environment got the courage to disobey an authority figure. The teacher was probably also perplexed, not having encountered a situation like this ever before. In any event, she said "Well, if you are not going to stand up on your chair, then I am going to ask you to leave the classroom (A subtle form of expulsion)." With that, my daughter came out of the class. Her aunt was called at home to come to the school and pick the child up.

As if that was not enough, my son got into a fist fight with one of his classmates. The details of the fist fight were not available. All I could get from my son was that he was punched by this other kid, probably an extreme form of bullying towards this "American" kid. My son promptly returned his punches and once again, his aunt, who was the local guardian for my children, was called and asked to take him home, at least for that day. Thus, it became obvious that these "American kids" would have to change their ways if they wanted to stay in school in India. After further discussion with their aunt (my late wife's sister), who also happened to be a physician, we decided that it would be probably quite traumatic for the children if we forced them to mend their ways to "fit" into the school, and it was better for us not to force it on them. Instead of that, we decided to let them enjoy their summer vacation and return to school in USA in the fall. Those two incidents in the school also sealed the decision once and for all that we will all return to USA for good.

While all this was going on, and strange though it might seem to many people in the West, I was literally hunting for a suitable wife through social contacts. There were no websites like "Match" or "eHarmony", or "it is just lunch" that I was aware of. Come to think of it, those people who are signed up on these sites are also "hunting" for a suitable partner. Thus, it is no different than what I was doing, except we might call these the modern version and more technologically advanced. There are now several websites to look for a partner and many of these cater to specific ethnic groups like "shaadi.com" or "gujratiwedding.com" which cater to Indians at large or smaller ethnic groups. Once again, I don't know if partners found through the websites lead to stable and successful marriages. Occasionally one comes across incidents where people put up a fake identity and many people have been defrauded into losing substantial sums of money (30). In any event, fortunately for me, we ran into the family of my present wife. Once again, my family and her family had known each other for three generations. My present father-in-law would relate to us stories how he used to visit the home of my grandparents. After meeting a couple of times, and my explaining to her what life would be in the USA and how difficult (or not so difficult) it would be to take care of the children, we both agreed to make a promise to make it work.

We got engaged, only a few days after I had first met her and I married Miss Ramma Dhamija on August 24,1979. Post marriage, the immediate problem was to get a passport for her, so we could get a visa for her to accompany me back to USA. Once again, my older brother came to rescue. He advised me to come to Chennai where he will be able to get a passport within a day whereas it would take us easily a few weeks before we could get a passport on our own.

Consequently, we cut down the days of our honeymoon and reached Chennai a few days after our marriage. The day after arrival, someone came from his office, took the passport application along with her photographs and in a matter of few hours delivered the passport to us. I have never seen or even heard an Indian Passport being delivered in such a short time.

Getting a visa from the American Embassy was another matter though. I was quite confident that getting a visa for her would not be a problem because I had gone through that process once before. We arrived at the US Embassy In New Delhi to obtain a visa, completed the application, and waited for a couple of hours, only to be told that a visa could not be issued because we did not have a marriage certificate to establish that Ramma and I were married, even though it clearly stated in her passport that her husband's name was Ved Gossain. (Indian Passports include the name of the husband or the name of the father of the passport holder). We were told to get a marriage certificate and reapply. The following day we went to the office of the registrar of marriages accompanied by her father and another relative, because two witnesses were required, besides the couple to obtain a certificate of marriage.

The following day we returned to the American Embassy and reapplied for a visa, only to be told that because of the backlog of applicants the Embassy was not issuing the visas on the same day as had been the practice until the previous week. They said that the application for the visa was approved and the visa will be available in a week or so. However, that one week became two weeks and then four weeks, such that there was no sight of a visa until it was time for me to return to the USA. The children and I therefore, left India, hoping that she will follow in a few days. But that was not to be. There was no information as to when her visa would arrive until it was almost Xmas time. During this time, we communicated by letters or phone and began getting to know each other a little more. By this time, we missed each other enough that I decided to go visit her in India for two weeks. (That is all the time I could get off from work) in the month of December 1979.

The visit was a good one, meeting her and the other family members. In retrospect, I think it was during this visit that I began to "love" her. She on the other hand has told me that she began to love me the day we were engaged.

While in India, once again we went back to the American embassy to check on the status of her visa, only to be told that it was being processed and there was nothing we could do to expedite the process.

On my return to the USA, I contacted the office of our senator, but once again I was told to be patient and the visa will arrive in due course of time. There was nothing more for us to do except wait. The visa did finally arrive in March 1980. I still remember the date that she arrived in the US (March 8, 1980).

The day before her arrival, I removed all the pictures of Veena that were in our house, practically in every room, so that she would have the feeling that she was entering the house of her husband and not that of another woman who lived there before her (Even though she was fully aware of the situation).

Almost immediately after her arrival here she began to take over the responsibilities of running a house. I remember that within a matter of a couple of days she fired the cleaning lady, that I had hired because she thought that the lady was "wasting her time" with watering the plants etc., rather than cleaning the house. Within a few days after her arrival, she also found the box where we had stored our family pictures, went through all the pictures and thereby was able to catch up with my life that had preceded her arrival. Although, I had told her all about that, anyway, but she was able to see that in pictures.

As mentioned before, marriages in India are not only a marriage between two people, but they are marriage of two families. The two families also agreed that this marriage was suitable and had a high chance of success. I might add now that their prophecy was correct. We have been happily married now for the last 40 years and continue to have a loving relationship. As expected in many arranged marriages, our love for each other continues to grow.

It took some time for the kids get to know her and for her to get to know the kids. However, I don't recall any major problems with the adjustment with the new composition of our family. Within about 6 months or so, the children began to address her and treat her as their mother. A few years later Ramma decided that she would like to adopt the children to make this relationship legal as well. We applied for the adoption. At the time of application, we had no idea that the process was somewhat complicated. We were visited by a social worker who met with the children separately, (away from us). At that time, the children were 12 and 13 years old. They must have confirmed that she indeed was as good as their "real" mother and the social worker must have confirmed that the relationship was a cordial and loving relationship, such that the adoption went through without a hitch.

I believe, my wife has been a good mother to my children from my previous marriage. We have added another child to our family, who has been nothing but a source of pleasure. I believe strongly that it was her support and her ability to provide a stable home environment, which has resulted in all three of our children maturing into successful adults. One of our sons is a physician, our daughter obtained an MBA and is now happily married to a fellow MBA graduate and has a 14-year-old son. Our youngest also obtained a master's degree in Business (MBA) and is now a health care administrator. Even though I say it myself, I think all the three children, now young adults, can be considered as having successful careers. I might also add that my present wife has given up many opportunities to advance her own career so that she could spend more time in looking after the children to make sure that the opportunities for their advancement were maximized. This would be no different than any biological parent would do for the benefit of his/her children. Thus, for all practical purposes, this is the only mother my children have known throughout their lives. I think, our daughter, who is a year older, seems to have a little more memory of her biological mother than our son. He does remember, his biological mother but has only vague memories of her.

I have never asked them how much they remember about their biological mother.

Our family (1990)

18

PRESERVING HER MEMORY

This brings me to discuss (or ask a question), how the memory of the deceased parent of young children should be preserved, and what role if any, it should play in their upbringing and day to day life? I don't think there is a right answer to this question. Each case must be handled on an individual basis. Many psychologists tell us that for the good mental health of the children, they should be told the truth. Most adoptive parents tell their adopted children that they were adopted. They may or may not tell them all the details of their biological parents and the circumstances under which they were adopted. Many adopted children, when they grow up as adults, want to know and go to extreme lengths to find their biological parents, whereas others are quite satisfied with their adoptive parents and make no effort to find their biological parents.

I have continued to question if we handled this aspect of her life, namely her memory correctly or not. I had no one to go to for advice, and I had no precedents to go by except one in our own family. One of my uncles had passed away before his son (my cousin) was born. This cousin of mine grew up in our joint extended family. For all practical purposes, my grandfather had adopted him (although not legally) and he did not know until he was in high school that our grandfather was not his biological father. In other words, he was not told that his father had died so that he would not suffer the trauma of the loss of his father. He grew up to be a successful adult and had a very successful and rewarding career, so I thought that it was a good model to follow. Therefore, we did not talk much about the biological mother of our children as they were very young, and I was not sure how they would handle that information. They grew up as if my second wife was their mother. As a matter of fact, our youngest child did not know for many years that his sister and brother were only his half-brother and sister. I might add, that all three of them are connected as well as any biological brother and sisters can be. However, I still sometimes wonder if that was the right model and perhaps her memory should have been a greater part of our lives than it has been. Perhaps one of these days, I will ask my older children (I have not had the courage so far) as to how we should have handled this aspect of their life or maybe they would tell me on their own. In any event, now that the children are all grown up adults, I have established a scholarship at the College of Human Medicine at the Michigan State University in her name which will keep her memory alive forever. I do derive a small satisfaction from this act.

Although the original author (Majumder), described the stages of acculturation of immigrants as being sequential, they most likely overlap, particularly the State of Struggle. As a matter of fact, I believe that the Stage of Struggle continues as long as one is alive. It may be no exaggeration to say, "Life is a struggle", immigrants or not.

19

PROFESSIONAL CAREER

About three years later (1981), it was time once again to apply for promotion to the rank of a full professor. Even though, some people might consider it "early ", I decided to apply for it any way since some other colleagues in the department with similar professional standing were applying. The promotion and reappointment (P&R) committee of the department recommended me for promotion. As is customary, the chair had requested letters of recommendations from outside the Michigan State University. After a thorough review of all the credentials, the chair decided not to support my promotion. He, therefore met with me to discuss the basis of his decision. He informed me that, although the P and R committee of the department had recommended promotion and the outside letters were strong, he could not "strongly" endorse it because he thought it was "too early" He went on to say that his advice was to wait for another year and next year "I will fight like a tiger to get it done for you." I readily accepted his advice and sure enough, the promotion went through smoothly without a hitch. In July of 1982, therefore, I became a full professor (with tenure). It was a happy and a proud moment for me since a childhood dream was fulfilled.

My performance at work must have been satisfactory or slightly better than that, because the chair at that time (Dr. Raymond Murray) decided that I was good enough for some additional administrative responsibilities, and he decided to appoint me as the Associate Chair of the Department. This appointment was confirmed by the members of the department without a single dissent. The appointment came with additional administrative responsibilities, but no additional monetary benefit. As a result of this appointment, I was now filling in for the chair, whenever he could not attend a meeting or whenever he wanted me to attend to a task or a meeting. I was also serving as the overall "Internal Medicine Clerkship Coordinator" for all students across all our affiliated communities. This also required quite a bit of travel across our affiliated communities, such as Grand Rapids, Flint, Saginaw and even Upper Peninsula, but I gladly did that thinking that it was advancing my professional career.

A couple of instances stand out in my memory in my role as the Associate Chair. The first one was to try and transfer one of our younger faculty (Michael Zaroukian) from a non-tenure position to a tenure track position. Mike was our up-and-coming star. I give credit to Dr. Murray for recognizing the potential of Dr. Zaroukian. It gave me an opportunity to learn more about the "tenure track" and the bureaucratic path needed to get there. It was a lot of work, but the outcome was rewarding in that Dr. Zaroukian was placed in the "tenure track". It was one of the best decisions that I participated in because Dr. Zaroukian went on to have a very successful academic career. Although he had obtained a Ph.D. in Immunology his chosen field became medical informatics and presently, he serves as the Chief Medical Information Officer, and a vice president at one of our affiliated hospitals.

The second incident arises from the fact that as the associate chair of the department, I now had the ability to access the salaries of the faculty members in our department. I was surprised to find out that there was a wide variation in the salaries that people at the same rank were bringing home. Somewhat more surprising was the discovery that there was an associate professor in the department, whose salary was even higher than a full professor in the department. Unfortunately, that full professor happened to be me. Naturally, I brought this fact to the attention of the chair. He responded by saying "I am not going to compare the salaries of individual faculty members but let us look at the history of your salary". We both reviewed the trajectory of my salary from the time of my appointment to the present time. The chair reminded me that I had always received at least an average (average for the department) but mostly above average raises. Thus, the conclusion was that I had been adequately compensated, and he refused to take any further action. I was disappointed and wondered if this was a kind of a discrimination. I might add that I had spent my lifetime counseling, younger minority faculty members and residents that bad things happen to people and every time something bad or what appears to be unfair occurs, they should not think that it was discrimination. However, having said that, every time some event happens that appears to be unfair, the immigrants or minorities wonder if it is discrimination or is it not. I must admit that I was not immune to similar feelings.

In any event, my response to this incident was to look for another job and fortunately a couple of months later, I was offered the position of "Chief of the Division of Endocrinology" at another medical school with a substantial salary raise. I brought this to the attention of my immediate supervisor (Dr. Rovner) and asked for his advice. His response "I do not know what you are going to do, but I know what I am going to do." When asked what, he said that he was going to see the dean right now, and he literally closed his brief case and left for the office of the dean. I don't know what they might have talked about, but that evening I got a call from the dean at my home. (Anecdotally, I might add, that was the only time that any dean has ever called me, and I have had the pleasure of working with every dean that the College of Human Medicine at MSU has had so far over a period of nearly 45 years). He almost pleaded with me to stay at MSU and promised a salary raise. I must admit that my "Indian values" prevailed and that is, it is more important to be wanted and valued at the place where you work, and the financial reward is secondary. I did get a small raise but nowhere near what I was being offered at the other place, but I gladly accepted it. In retrospect, I realize that it is not the "American way". I should have negotiated hard and tried to get as much a raise as I could but did not. It is because of my inability or lack of desire to negotiate hard, that one of my colleagues would later tell me "Ved! You have a "character defect". When asked to elaborate, she would say that "you don't stand up for your rights". As I look back, I must agree with her assessment. There were several opportunities along the way where a better negotiator could have (would have) received a better deal than I was able to. I also realize now that there are special courses and experts from whom one could learn the art of negotiation. I used to think that these courses and experts were in the business to make money for themselves and the participants don't learn much from these courses. However, I wonder now if they are helpful. If I had an opportunity to do it over, I would certainly explore that option. I should mention that I did attend one such course designed for the Chiefs of the department of Medicine while I was an associate chair. The only thing that I learned from this three-day course for a tuition fee of $2,500 (in the year 1982), is that when your chief asks you to take on additional responsibility (or responsibilities) you should not immediately say Yes or No. Instead, ask for some time to think about it, by saying, "let us sleep over it tonight" and when you have thought about it and if you want to take on the additional responsibilities, ask what else can you drop or what monetary additional compensation will you get. (By the way the latter i.e., negotiation was not mentioned in the course, but I have learned that from experience). The course leaders also mentioned that when you become a leader of a department, it is not about you anymore. Your main job and the energies you spend are for the progress of your department and the team members that you are leading. In other words, you sacrifice your personal advancement, or personal benefit for the sake of your team. That approach is clearly idealistic and morally very satisfying to the individual, but I am not sure, how well that is appreciated by others. I would later find out that this approach clearly comes at a personal cost.

As I was exploring the option of going to this other medical school, I ran into a faculty member who had previously served at that institution, which I was considering but had returned to MSU.

I informed him that I had been offered the job of the chief of the division of Endocrinology and if I should accept that position. His first question to me was, "Do you want to go to this redneck area?" I must admit that at that time (it was 1984), I did not even know what a "redneck" meant. So, I asked others and tried to learn more about the concept of redneck. "The definition of a redneck is a slang and derogatory term for a poor white person, often who lives in the rural Southern United States and who often has a provincial conservative or often bigoted attitude" (The American Heritage Dictionary of English language, 5th edition 2013). It was this understanding of red neck, that also made me somewhat circumspect about accepting this job. But it was clearly the persuasion of Dr. Rovner and the dean that lead to my decision about continuing to stay at MSU and even in retrospect, I have no regrets about that decision. My further journey at MSU has been personally and professionally rewarding.

Another interesting event occurred after several years of my appointment at MSU, i.e., that the administration of the medical school decided that they wanted to re-verify my credentials. These had been checked at the time of my initial appointment. For this purpose, they asked me to produce original certificates of my medical school diploma, proof of residency and fellowship training. There was no problem finding those documents and submitting it to the administration, except for one, namely the original MB,BS degree. For some reason, I just could not find that, although I had several photocopies of that document. The photocopies, however, were not acceptable and that was quite a change from the time I had entered United States, when the photocopies of my MB,BS degree and other documents were considered as good as original. I argued that if my credentials were not genuine, several medical students had "passed" their medical clerkship and thereby graduated from MSU over my signature and thus their documents could also be considered as not genuine. Fortunately, the administration did not make a big deal out of it but still wanted me to produce the original degree in the near future. A few weeks later, I was in Chandigarh India, where I had been invited to give a presentation at the annual meeting of the

Endocrine Society of India. I asked a colleague there, how I could obtain a duplicate copy of my MB,BS degree, and he suggested that we ask the Vice Chancellor of Punjab University who would be present later in the evening at a reception. (Punjab University was the body that had issued the original MBBS degree and is located in Chandigarh). We did exactly that and he (The Vice Chancellor) suggested, that if a faculty member at the Post Graduate Institute of Medical Education and Research Chandigarh (PGIMER) could testify that I had attended the medical school and I could provide the details, a duplicate could be issued at a nominal cost of 300 Rupees (About 4 dollars in today's money). A classmate of mine, who was now a senior faculty member at PGIMER was able to testify that I had attended Medical college Amritsar along with him for all five years and had successfully passed all the professional examinations required by the college and the university. He also paid the amount required for the duplicate copy of the degree. Thus, I was able to get a duplicate degree almost effortlessly, whereas I had been thinking that it would be a monumental task, if not impossible to get a duplicate copy of the degree nearly 20 years after graduation, another example of good luck. As luck would have it, after I received the duplicate, I was able to find the original degree also, precisely where it should have been. Although, I had earlier searched that folder several times but could not find it. In any event, the important point is that I was able to satisfy the administration that I had indeed graduated from a medical school and my basic medical degree (MB,BS) was genuine.

When Dr Murray stepped down from the chairman ship of the department in 1989 another faculty member (Late Dr Greenbaum) was appointed as the interim chair. He asked me to continue to serve as the associate chair and I did. About two years later we had a new chair for the department. On his arrival, I offered to resign my position as the "associate chair" as a matter of protocol. He, however, asked me to continue to stay on as the associate chair for the Lansing community and Dr Greenbaum was appointed associate chair for the affiliated communities outside of Lansing. In 1994, when the program director of the Internal Medicine residency program decided to leave MSU, the chair asked me take over as the program director of this program. We both agreed that I would only serve as an interim program director for one year. After the retirement of Dr Rovner in 1996, I was appointed the chief of the division of Endocrinology, another appointment that I am particularly proud of, because in my mind it was indicative of recognition of my ability and skills as an Endocrinologist at a national level.

20
STAGE OF DOUBT

The stage of "Struggle" transitions into stage of "Anxiety" or stage of "Doubt". During this stage, the immigrants begin to have doubts about the decision they have made. Multiple questions begin to pop up. "Have I made the right decision by staying here? How will my children grow up here? What kind of adults will they become? Who will they marry? How will I react if they decide to marry someone that I don't particularly approve of? Where will they get any religious education about the religion that I follow?" At that time, as already mentioned, there were no Hindu Temples in the country. Many Hindu families that I knew, tilted towards the Mormon philosophy as this was, in their opinion, more closely aligned to the Hindu philosophy. Many families began to take a more broad-minded view of religion and decided to expose their children to multiple religions, sticking to the philosophy that all religions basically teach the same things. By exposing the children to different religious philosophies, they had hoped that their children will grow up to be more informed adults and better human beings. To the best of my knowledge, there are no data to support or refute this claim.

There are concerns that mainly revolve around the future of the children. What will my children do for a living? Will they pursue a career as a professional, i.e., will they go to college, pursue a graduate degree, or simply settle down as a "blue collar" worker after high school. It is obvious that the immigrant parents, like any other set of parents, want and hope that their children will do better in life than the parents themselves have done. Most of the immigrants that I had contact with were professionals, such as Physicians and Engineers. Consequently, a blue-collar career was not, what they had wanted for their children. The next concern is who will they marry? Will they marry someone from their own culture and background, or will they marry someone from an entirely different background and culture. Implied in this doubt is also how will they go about finding their life partner, i.e., by dating in an entirely western way or will they even consider an "arranged" marriage or something in between. The main concern the parents have is, whether they will have any say in the process of selection or in the final outcome, namely who their children pick as their life partners.

As the Indian community has matured in the USA many interracial marriages have taken place, where one member of the couple is of Indian origin and the other is not. In our own case our two sons have married two Caucasian women, whereas our daughter is married to a fellow of Indian descent, whose parents like us are first generation immigrants from India.

It should also be mentioned that the first generation of immigrants have a very strong desire to maintain their culture, and they want to leave their culture and their traditions for the future generations to the largest extent possible. That is one reason we have seen such a proliferation of religious institutions such as Hindu temples, mosques (for Muslims) and Gurdwaras (for Sikh religion).

When Majumdar described the stages of acculturation of Indian immigrants in 1986, the migration of Indians to the US was relatively new phenomenon. As a result, the "Stage of Doubt" was more of a theoretical concern, rather than a practical one. However, over the last 30 to 40 years or so, these doubts have begun to take real shape. Many of the children of Indian immigrants have married outside of their culture and ethnic backgrounds. Most of them, (if not all of them) have adopted the western system of dating and even cohabitation for months or years before deciding if they want to marry the person with whom they have lived, much to the dismay of their parents. While this may be good for assimilation into the culture of their adopted country, this often does not meet the approval of their parents. The parents, although they may disapprove or even condemn this process, find themselves helpless to intervene or in any way to change the course of events. Needless to add that this is a source of great deal of anguish and frustration for many of the parents.

While these doubts remain in the background, most people continue to follow the career path that they have chosen for themselves. In academic medicine, this usually means development of new and innovative programs, obtaining outside funding for research and publishing the findings of their research in reputable journals. The higher the "impact" factor of the journal, the better it is for the authors of the article.

One such opportunity came our way in mid-1980s. One of our affiliated hospitals was approached by a pharmaceutical company to develop a "weight management center", using a commercial product, which had been shown to result in substantial weight loss. To carry out this program, the hospital needed an Endocrinologist to medically supervise the program. The hospital approached the department of Medicine at the University and a contract was negotiated that the department provide a physician who would serve as the "Medical Director" of the program. Besides the medical director, the department also agreed to provide other physicians, most of whom would be University employees, but they would work with the medical director (an Endocrinologist) and would be compensated for their professional effort. The medical director would receive a stipend for his/her effort, but the hospital would own the program. This appeared to be a win-win situation for both parties. The department will not have to come up with any capital expenses but would receive the monies for the professional services of the physicians and the money received by the department for the medical directorship could be used to hire an additional faculty member or a trainee. The hospital will own the program because it would be responsible for the facilities, marketing and maintaining the program and hiring additional staff as needed. I was appointed as the medical director of the program and as it turned out, we ended up hiring a trainee (fellow) in Endocrinology funded by the compensation received for my services as the medical director of the program. I should also add that the total compensation received by the medical director did not change my personal salary, once again a reflection of my inability to negotiate for myself. As one might expect, we put in a lot of time and effort in getting the program off the ground, marketing it, showing good results. But it might be said that it was all worth the effort because it developed into a successful program both from a medical and financial standpoint. In this program, on the average, women lost about 20 Kg, and men lost about 30 Kg of weight in about 6 months and those who stayed with the program were able to maintain it for at least a year. The program also provided many opportunities for research and we were able to publish several articles relating to the management of obesity and the benefits of rapid weight loss. A few years later when the program was running on an "automatic pilot", the hospital decided that they did not need (or want) the department, or the University employed medical director and simply decided not to renew the contract. Fortunately, from the point of view of individual physicians, this had no major impact, but collectively for the department and the college, who had put in a lot of effort in the development of this program, the major consequence was that we had nothing to show for our work. The work we had done collectively was handed over to the hospital on a silver platter. For me personally, this was a major disappointment because I had spent a lot of time and energy on this project.

While this was going on, we began to negotiate with another hospital in town to develop a "Diabetes Treatment Center". It is well known that the MSU-College of Human Medicine is a University based community medical school and does not have its own hospital. As a matter of fact, it was one of the first such community based medical school. In those days, there used to be a chain of "Diabetes Centers in America" much along the lines of "Cancer Center of America". They would provide an infrastructure and some background material, but the care will be provided by local physicians and nurses. The negotiation process went well for about a year, and we were told that the contract will be signed by noon tomorrow. However, that tomorrow never came, and the negotiations broke down at the last minute. Once again, it was a major disappointment because a lot of effort had been spent in preparing for this arrangement and through this center, we were hoping to provide the "state of art" care for people with diabetes in our community, which I thought was badly needed, but would not be possible now.

A few months later, another hospital (the same with which we had collaborated to develop the weight management center) approached us to develop a "Diabetes Treatment Center". The hospital already had a rudimentary "diabetes education" program in that there were two diabetes educators who provided diabetes related education to patients that were admitted to the hospital. As the word of this got out, we were approached by Joslin Clinic, Mayo Clinic, and the Diabetes Center in Minneapolis, Minnesota to adopt their programs. These institutions would give us their name and some background material, but the care would be provided by local physicians, nurses, and diabetes educators. In return, these institutions would charge us a substantial amount of money for the use of their name. We visited a few of these institutions and some others and concluded that we had all the expertise needed, and we could embark upon the development of a Diabetes Center, without any help from outside agencies.

So, after several years of meetings between the members of the division of Endocrinology (Department of Medicine at Michigan State University) and the members of the hospital, mainly a diabetes educator and a midlevel administrator, a regional diabetes center was finally established in 1997. An Endocrinologist in private practice and a member of the hospital staff was appointed the medical director. Although the diabetes center was now established with a medical director, full staffing of diabetes educators, nurses, and secretaries not many patients were being seen there, most likely because the only physician affiliated with the center was its medical director, who had his own private practice as his main business. Since the diabetes center would be competing for patients with his own private patients, perhaps it was not in his best personal financial interest to increase the patient load at the diabetes center. Although, I do not (and did not) have access to the financial situation of the diabetes center, it was apparent that the center would not have been a profitable business at that time. A couple of years later, the administration of the hospital approached the Chair of the Department of Medicine at the University and convinced him that we should support the diabetes center and begin seeing patients with diabetes at the center. The chair asked me to support the center any way I could. Consequently, I transferred my established practice of diabetes of more than 25 years to the diabetes center in the year 2000. By this time, I had already become the chief of the division of Endocrinology in the department of Medicine at the University. As a result of that, we were able to add other faculty members, members of the Endocrine Division of the University to work at the center. Thus, collectively, we were seeing many patients with diabetes and even some with other endocrine disorders. As a result of this increased manpower and the reputation of University physicians, the center was functioning at its full capacity and patients were having to wait for 2-3 months to get an appointment.

We, the physicians working in the diabetes center, in collaboration with medical director, and the administrative director of the center, wanted to start an inpatient diabetes service, which would not only provide a much-needed service for patients, but also provide an opportunity to train younger physicians, auxiliary medical staff, education and even research. Moreover, it would be a profit generating service for the hospital. We developed a plan for the development of an inpatient diabetes service. I was given the task, by the group to present our plan to the medical staff executive committee, which approved it unanimously. The executive committee also asked the hospital to provide more resources than we had asked for (we had asked for one nurse practitioner while the executive committee suggested that we should at least have two). Although the plan now had the support of medical staff executive committee, the hospital did not put any resources behind it, for reasons best known to the administration. A few months later the medical director also resigned his position, but no specific reason was mentioned for this action. The hospital once again turned to the department of medicine, looking for a medical director, since all the Endocrinologists in town were employed by the university. The hospital wanted a medical director who would spend 80% of his/her time at the diabetes center, so that there would be more continuity of care for the patients that were being seen there. It was agreed to appoint one of the faculty members from the division of Endocrinology as the medical director. As the Chief of Endocrine Section, at that time, I was not in favor of this arrangement. I was concerned that we will essentially be giving one of our faculty to the hospital, who will not be available to teach or see patients at the University or be able to contribute to research, but I was overruled by the chair, and the chief executive officer of the Health Team (Health Team was the entity that managed the practice by the University physicians). However, unfortunately, this collaborative arrangement did not last long. One of the mandates for the newly appointed medical director was to initiate and implement an inpatient diabetes service, based on the plan already outlined. To his credit, the newly appointed medical director made a sincere effort to begin a medically sound inpatient diabetes service, but the medical director and the Vice President of the center had different ideas as to how the program would be implemented. Apparently the two could not come to an agreement. The consequence of this plan was a "divorce" between the hospital and the department of Medicine at the University. Currently the regional diabetes center is staffed entirely by the hospital employed physicians, nurse practitioners and other ancillary staff and the MSU division of Endocrinology runs its own practice on the University premises. Collaboration between the two programs would have been so much more beneficial to the community and I believe, also for both institutions. Instead of that, they now compete.

These are just two examples that I have personally experienced about the relationship of this hospital and the department of medicine at the Michigan State University. Both these programs were successful for a "short term". By that I mean, that although, they lasted for several years, but they could not be sustained for longer periods, or forever. The University (MSU) and the hospital continue to maintain an ongoing relationship because they clearly need each other. I believe, the two institutions have signed a memo of understanding to cooperate. But they are two independent institutions and in some instances the interests of the institution rather than the collaborative benefits become the dominant factor in negotiations. As a result, many programs don't get off the ground or are discontinued after a variable period (See above). Many of these contracts are negotiated at the unit level, which makes me wonder that if these negotiations were held at the highest level of both institutions, the results might be different. In all fairness, there are several programs, which are collaboratively run and have been very successful, such as the Trauma program, stroke services, neonatology and some residency programs and others that I may not be aware of. A few years later, an MSU sponsored, but hospital supported (financially) cardiology fellowship program was launched, which continues to be a successful program. More recently, the hospital has sponsored additional fellowship programs in Endocrinology and Infectious diseases in collaboration with the university which are quite successful.

21

ESTABLISHING ENDOCRINOLOGY FELLOWSHIP

As mentioned above, one of the reasons for the physician shortage in this country is that the number of residency slots is limited. However, approximately in the year 2004, the US government decided that in certain areas, the training positions for young physicians could be increased, and our area also happened to be included in this program. Therefore, the Department of Medicine at MSU decided to develop fellowships in Endocrinology and Infectious Diseases in collaboration with the same hospital.

For the training of the fellows a clinical site (a hospital) is essential and since MSU does not have its own hospital a collaborative arrangement is essential to carry out a training program. It is also important to mention at this point, that developing a fellowship program and getting it approved had become much more complex compared to a few years previous. We had fellows in the 1990's and at that time, the only requirement to have a fellowship program was that the institution should have an approved internal medicine residency program (approved by the American Board of Internal Medicine). However, in 2004, it required a very detailed application, describing the facilities, both clinical and academic, faculty, not only in the specific subspecialty, but also in the entire Department of Medicine, a detailed outline of the curriculum, right down to the details of how many clinics will the fellows attend, how will they be supervised, how much time they will spend in the hospital and how often they will be on call, etc., etc. We completed a very long application and submitted it in December 2004. After that, it was wait and see. If the application was approved, the institution and the program will be site visited by representatives of the American Board of Internal Medicine (ABIM) following which they will submit their report to the residency review committee (RRC), who will make the final decision whether the fellowship was "accredited" or not. The application was approved, and we were given a date for the site visit.

Happily, the outcome of our site visit and the decision of the Residency Review Committee was favorable, and both the Endocrinology and Infectious Diseases (ID) fellowships were approved. We were notified in September/October of the year 2005 that the fellowship in Endocrinology was approved retrospectively from July 2005. So, we had the option to recruit a fellow immediately or in January 2006, but we decided to remain synchronized with the academic calendar year and opted to wait until July of 2006 to recruit our first fellow.

It is also interesting to note that recruitment of the fellows in those days was much simpler than it is today. The fact that the fellowship was available was mentioned in the "Green book", which lists all the training positions available in the US. We received several applications. We interviewed a few candidates and narrowed our choice to two candidates, but we had only one position to offer. After a great deal of difficulty in arriving at the final decision, we offered the position to one candidate, who readily accepted, only to let us know, a few weeks later that because her mother's health was failing and that she would like to begin her fellowship in 2007 instead of 2006. This allowed us to recruit our equally good second choice for the year 2006. Thus, in one stroke, we were able to recruit two candidates for the first two years of the program. The process is much more complicated now because like the residents, the fellows are also recruited through the "Match" program. In this process, the applicants rank the institutions that they interview at and the program ranks the candidates. The computer then "matches" the candidates with the institutions. Consequently, until the results are announced, neither the candidate knows where he/she will end up going, nor the institution knows who will come into their program.

Getting the program off the ground and making sure it would be a successful program required a lot of work. We were trying to achieve a balance between the "service" activities that the fellows would participate in but making sure they had time for educational activities as well as opportunities for scholarly pursuits. I still remember telling our first fellow that she probably could have gone to some high powered, well established institution, such as Yale or Harvard, but she would not have 3 faculty members teaching a single fellow. The fellowship program has done well and is now considered a very respectable program among Endocrinology fellowships around the country.

In about 2008, we switched to participating in the "Match program". Once again, as we applied for renewal of fellowship program, I discovered that my salary was much lower compared to the other program directors, who were much junior in the academic rank but happened to be white males, and once again it brought up the age-old question, is it discrimination? When I told this to our chair, she gave me a "small raise" instantaneously. Although, the raise was clearly small, I did not or could not say anything. To make matters worse for me, that is the raise I would have got as part of my annual raise any way. At this point, although, I considered filing a "grievance", but ultimately, decided not to fight it. MSU, like many other institutions in the US, is an "equal opportunity employer", but in my opinion, the discrimination at MSU and the US is alive and well, and it comes in all kinds of flavors. However, this is not unique to MSU. It has previously been described that minority faculty are less likely to be promoted to senior ranks than white faculty. (31).In a study of the faculties of 24 medical schools, Peterson et al observed that 63% of underrepresented minority faculty (URM) and 50% of non-underrepresented (NURM) minority faculty perceived racial and ethnic bias or obstacles to career success or satisfaction compared to

29% of majority faculty. Nearly half (48%) of URM and 26% of NURM reported personally encountering racial/ethnic discrimination by a superior or a colleague compared to 7 % of majority faculty (32). If there was no discrimination in the nation, how come we have incidents like Ferguson, Missouri, where an unarmed teenager Michael Brown was killed on Aug 9,2014. The shooting prompted protests that roiled the area for weeks. Incidents like demonstrations commemorating the killing of Michael Brown one year ago ended when an 18-year-old was shot and critically wounded by the police (33). In Charleston, South Carolina 9 black people were killed in a church. The police chief called it a "hate crime" (34), and movements like "Black Lives Matter". More recently the death of George Floyd, a black American at the hands of a white police officer led to nationwide protests (35). Although, the country has received much attention related to "Black Lives Matter", other instances of racism have not. For example, Chicago police shot a Sikh gentleman, and in Alabama, an elderly Indian immigrant was tackled to the floor and handled ruthlessly by the police to the point that he was admitted to the ICU of a local hospital. His only fault was that he did not speak English and therefore could not explain to the police why he was walking in that neighborhood which happened to be the neighborhood where his son lived. This gentleman had travelled all the way from India to be with his son and grandchildren. These two lives were equally important, but we have not seen much about those in the media, which makes me ask the question, "Does media discriminate too?" But I am in no position to establish that one way or the other. But right now, we are talking about discrimination at academic centers.

As recently as Jan 2020 Afua Hirsch, a black British journalist who also teaches Journalism at the university of Southern California wrote "No matter how beautiful you are, whom you marry, what palaces you occupy, charities you support, how faithful you are, how much money you accumulate or what good deeds you perform, in this society racism will still follow you" (36).

Nicholas Kristof (37) wrote a series of columns in New York times "When Whites Just Don't Get It" about racial inequity, and one of the most common responses from angry whites was along the lines: This stuff about white privilege is nonsense and if blacks lag, the reason lies in the black community. Just look at Asian Americans. Those Koreans and Chinese make it in America because they work hard. All people can succeed here if they stop whining and start working. While by many standards, I would consider my academic life at MSU a success, I do feel that I have not been rewarded academically and financially in an equitable manner. Along the way, there were opportunities for me to become the chair of our department. As a matter of fact, on one occasion, the departing chair had recommended to the dean that I would be a good candidate for the position of the "acting chair "until a permanent chair could be appointed. The dean, however, chose to ignore that recommendation and asked another faculty member who was planning to retire, to postpone his retirement and stay on as an acting chair. On another occasion when there was an opening for the position of the chair of the department, the dean asked me to serve on the "search committee" for the selection of the chair. An unwritten rule of the University is that if you are serving on the "search committee", you are automatically excluded from being a candidate for the position. I suppose, I could have declined to serve on the search committee but rightly or wrongly, I took this request from the dean to also mean that he would not like me to be a candidate for the position of the chair. A few years later there was once again, an opportunity to serve as the "acting chair". Several members of the department met with the dean (this time a different dean) to discuss the process of selecting an "acting Chair" for the department. One of the faculty who had previously served as an acting chair in the past, once again expressed his interest to serve in that role. At this point another faculty member suggested that I should be considered for that position. The, dean asked me if I would like to be considered for that position and I responded, "Under certain circumstances I would very much like to be considered for this position". However, there was no further communication with me, and I was not selected. Another junior, non-tenured person was appointed. Coincidentally, he happened to be a white male. It is partly, or may be mostly my own fault, I did not fight for what I thought I deserved, or I did not stand up for myself, perhaps a manifestation of the "character defect" that I have, as mentioned to me earlier by a colleague. It is entirely possible that I may not have had the qualifications or other attributes to be the chair of an academically important department in the college, I find that hard to believe, because I had served as the associate Chair of the department for about 6 years and the person who was appointed as the "acting chair" had no administrative experience. Under the circumstances, it is difficult, if not impossible, not to wonder, if the color of my skin, or the country of my origin, or the foreign medical school I had attended were responsible for this "discrimination."

Being Asian myself, I agree with Kristof (New York Times Digest, October 11, 2015) when he asks the question "Does success of Asian Americans suggest the age of discrimination is behind us?" He sums it up by stating "Sure! Let's celebrate the success of Asian Americans and emulate the respect for education and strong families. But let's not use the success of Asians to pat ourselves on the back and pretend that discrimination is history".

22

AWARDS

My journey through MSU has not been a story of struggle and discrimination only, but I have also been rewarded by a few awards. As mentioned above, I had already received a "fellowship" In the American College of physicians, prior to coming to MSU. The Royal college of Physicians of Canada also bestowed their fellowship which was by virtue of an exam which I had completed. A fellowship in the American college of Endocrinologists was awarded in the year 2000. Later in the year 2016, I was awarded "The outstanding Endocrinologist award" by the American Association of Clinical Endocrinologists. The AACE Outstanding Clinical Endocrinologist Award is presented to an AACE member practicing in the United States, in recognition of dedicated and compassionate care provided to patients with endocrine diseases, exceptional knowledge and expertise in the field of clinical endocrinology, and active advocacy of AACE's mission in both professional and public environments. I had remained engaged with professional organizations back home in India and received the "Prof Vishwanathan oration award" in the year 2000 by the research Society of Diabetes in India (RSSDI), an organization which was founded by my mentor Professor Ahuja and is now the premier society for the study of Diabetes in India. (Professor Vishwanathan was a highly respected Endocrinologist in India). Subsequently, the ACP

(Michigan chapter) awarded me the "Laureate award" in 2004 and this was followed by the award of Mastership in the ACP in 2014."The Laureate Award is designed to honor those Fellows and Masters of the College who have demonstrated, by their example and conduct, an abiding commitment to excellence in medical care, education, and research, and service to their community, their chapter, and the ACP. A Laureate nominee is usually a senior physician who is: 1) Fellow or Master of the College 2) Achieved a long history of excellence and peer approval in the specialty of internal medicine. 3) Served the chapter and community with distinction or in some clearly definable manner, whereas the Mastership in the college (MACP) is awarded to the Fellows who have been selected because of "integrity, positions of honor, eminence in practice or in medical research, or other attainments in science or in the art of medicine." Masters must be highly accomplished persons demonstrating eminence in practice, leadership, or in medical research. The Master must be distinguished by the excellence and significance of his or her contributions to the field of medicine. (ACP by laws). Thus, it is one of the highest honors that the college can bestow on its members, who are "fellows". The endowed professorship "Swartz professor" that I received in 2005 and the distinguished faculty award that I received from the college of Human Medicine that in 2006 are the other honors that I count as indicators of my success at MSU, and I am very proud of those. I mention these, only to indicate that some achievements have been recognized at MSU and by the external Organizations such as the American college of physicians and the American association of Clinical Endocrinologists.

I am sure, that I would have not reached this level of success without the facilities, help and support that I have received at MSU, and for that I am immensely thankful to several hundred medical students, many residents and fellows and several faculty colleagues mostly at MSU but also at other institutions as well with whom I had collaborated over the years.

Accepting the AACE award for "Outstanding Endocrinologist"

23

LIFE CHANGING EVENT

A trivial event, but with possible serious consequences, changed the trajectory of my life. I slipped on ice (slipping on ice in Michigan is a common happening) and hit the back of my head on the edge of the step on my front door. Immediately after the fall, I felt well except for the pain in the back of my head. After a few minutes of rest, I was ready to go to work and did go to work. As a matter of fact, on my way to work, I was able to help a neighbor who had also fallen on the ice on the same day. Her husband was out of town. So, she had called me to let me know that she had fallen and that her hand was swollen. I responded "OK, I will stop by at your place before I go to work." The streets and her entire driveway were simply a sheet of ice. I had to drive on her driveway as close to the garage door as I could, then holding on to the car I walked into her house. One look at her hand convinced me that she had fractured her wrist. She, therefore needed X rays and possible surgery to fix the broken bone. I drove her to the clinic where the x rays confirmed the fracture. We then drove to the office of an Orthopedic surgeon who was known to me and he promised to take care of her. I felt OK during the rest of the day. However, the following morning, I noticed the worst vertigo (Sense of spinning) of my life. I could not stand up, felt nauseated, but did not vomit. My wife called our neighbor, a neurologist who lived across the street from us. At 6 am, he was kind enough to come over, examined me, and the differential diagnosis he was pronouncing scared me more than the fall. He said the possibilities are cerebellar hemorrhage (brain hemorrhage) with or without subdural hematoma (Collection of blood under the skull bone) vertebral artery dissections (tear in one of the main arteries to the brain). At first, he said that we could wait and get MRI later in the day, but a couple of hours later, he changed his mind, called us back and said that we should come to the emergency room (ER), where diagnostic and therapeutic (treatment) evaluations could be done. My wife decided to drive me to the hospital; even though I could not stand up and had to lie down on the back seat of the car. The neurologist friend (Dr Narendra Patel) met us in the ER and promptly arranged for a CT, which fortunately showed no signs of a bleed in the brain. I was admitted and the following day, the MRI also did not reveal any lesions of any consequence. So, two days later, I was discharged home but with a walker because I was still unstable on my feet. The thought of having to walk with the help of a walker was really a very scary one. I began to think "what if I have to walk with a walker for the rest of my life?" I must admit, that over the course of my medical career, I must have seen many people walk with a walker and some of these were even prescribed by me. On those occasions it did not seem to matter. However, when it affects one's own self, it has a completely different impact. The instability of the gait fortunately did not persist for long, and I was able to get rid of the walker in a few days. Nevertheless, we made the decision that we were no longer going to spend the winters in Michigan. I approached the chair, and she was agreeable that we will change my appointment to an "academic year", but I will be able to take 3 months off in the winter semester rather than getting summers off, as was customary with academic year appointments. We did that for the years 2011 through 2014. She also asked me if I wanted to "retire", and I said, "If you can find someone suitable to take my position as the chief of the Endocrinology division, I will step down as the chief of the section".

She – Then what?
Me – I would like to work part-time (approximately 50% time)
She – That would be fine.

However, we did not put anything in writing. Nevertheless, unbeknown to me, she put in an advertisement looking for a section Chief of Endocrinology. Thus, the effort to recruit a new chief of the division was on. This decision by her would have a significant effect on my retirement plans. (See later).

24

STAGE OF GIVING

Although, in the original description of the stages of Acculturation, Majumdar described these stages as being sequential, they are not necessarily so. One such event at MSU was the establishment of the "India Council" at MSU. MSU has many International programs and centers such as African study center and Asia study center. Under the Asia study center there were established China and Japan Council for the study of their respective countries. Back in 1987, there was no India Council. I happened to be at a seminar at the International center, where the late professor Kannapan, a professor of Economics, who had just returned from India after a sabbatical there, was giving a presentation. At the end of the presentation, the then dean commented that such presentation would be best held under the auspices of India Council, but unfortunately, we don't have one. When asked to further elaborate as to why we don't have one, he went on to say, that the councils can only be established if there is faculty, as well as support from the community. We tried a few years ago but the Indian Community in this town is so split that they would not (could not) come together to support this venture. I don't know why, but I took his comments as "offensive", perhaps because I thought, that this did not reflect well on the Indian community of the Lansing area of which I was also a member. I asked him: what would it take to get the India Council "endowed "?

Dean; 20,000 dollars (that is all it took in those days. Now a days, I think it is up to 50,000 dollars)
Me; over what time period
Dean; Over 5 years.
Me: consider it done in one year's time.

I thought, it should be no problem to raise that much money from our community in one year's time. I, therefore, took it upon myself to go ahead and start raising funds. Not having done any fundraising in my life, I discovered that, it was a lot harder than I had imagined, but we were finally able to establish the "India Council" in the Asia study center in 1989 and I served as the director of the council for several years. I might add that it has continued to do well and remains well established, and it continues to sponsor India related academic and cultural programs.

By this time, I was also reaching the final stage in the life of an immigrant, i.e., "Stage of Giving". The immigrants, having spent a large part of their life in their adopted land, now begin to think about giving something back to the society they have lived in. There is also a desire to leave behind their culture and religion for future generations. That is why we have been witnessing a proliferation of Hindu temples, Muslim Mosques, and Sikh gurudwaras in the US. Many a cultural event are also held in these places of worship.

It was also time to give back to my profession. I had been the program director of the Endocrinology fellowship since it was established in 2006.After about 7 years of being program director, I thought it was important for me to step down and have a younger colleague take over in the spirit of looking out for the division or the department rather than advancing myself. Consequently, I stepped down from the position of the Program director in the year 2013 and passed it on to a younger colleague, who although officially was not designated as the "Associate program director", had been training for the position. The program has continued to do well, and we have matched every year until 2015. In the last couple of years, the match results have not been so favorable. This, in my opinion, does not reflect that the program is anyway less rigorous than in the years gone by, but shows the unpredictability of the new match program. One of the measures that the American Board of Internal Medicine (ABIM) uses to determine the success of the program is the pass rates on the subspecialty board exams, and I am proud to say that so far, the pass rate among our fellows has been 100%.

I had been a member of our county medical society, the state medical society and the American Medical Association (AMA) almost ever since I arrived in Lansing, Michigan (1975) but had been an inactive member, because I had concentrated mainly on my academic career. During this time there had been a lot of changes in the medical profession including how physicians were being reimbursed as well as other laws that had been introduced affecting the practice of Medicine. I felt that it was time to get involved in advocacy for the profession.

I, therefore, contested for and was elected the secretary, president elect and ultimately as the president of our county medical society. That gave me an opportunity to get involved in the medical affairs at the state level. I still serve as one of the delegates to the Michigan State medical society from our county. Although the discrimination against the foreign medical graduates (now called International Medical graduates or IMGs) had significantly decreased over the years, a section for IMGS still existed at the American Medical association, the purpose of which is to represent the IMG community to the House of Delegates of AMA, where all the policy decisions of the AMA are made. I decided to run for a seat on the Governing council of the IMG section and was elected to be a member of the governing council for the section of International Medical Graduates (IMGs) and ultimately served as the chair of the governing council. Once I got on the governing council, I realized that the issues for the IMGs had not changed much since I arrived in this country, almost 50 years ago.

The IMGs constitute about 25% of the practicing physicians and about 28% residents are IMGs (Source AMA). There is also a predicted shortage of the physicians in the USA. The Association of American

Medical Colleges (AAMC)has stated that the United States will see a shortage of up to nearly 122,000 physicians by 2032 as demand for physicians continues to grow faster than supply. According to new data published by the AAMC, the projected shortfall is like the past projections and ranges from 46,900 to 121,900 physicians. (AAMC news April 23,2019).

Despite this, there are many IMGs who are eligible to enter the residency programs (Certified by Educational Commission of Foreign Medical Graduates (ECFMG)), but are unable to do so, because the number of residency spots are capped at the level, they were in 1997. The residencies are supported by funding from the Medicare programs and there has not been an increase in funding. In the recent years, this problem has been aggravated, by an increase in the number of US medical schools, and by the proliferation of medical schools for profit in the Caribbean, often called "offshore medical schools". These schools admit students, who are mostly US citizens, with the promise of getting them residency position in the USA. They complete the first two years of their medical education in their parent medical schools and most of the Clerkships (Clinical rotations) are arranged in the USA. Sometimes the students can find a clerkship spot on their own, and at other times these clerkship spots are arranged by the medical school itself, for which the parent medical school pays the hospitals that accept their medical students. The teaching of these students is done by the volunteer US physicians who are part of the hospital staff. Some of these hospitals are "teaching" hospitals, where many US medical students also train. This sometimes leads to the displacement of the US medical students because the hospitals prefer to take the students from offshore medical schools since it adds to their bottom line because of the revenue received from the offshore medical schools for training their students. On the other hand, in many instances these hospitals are nonteaching hospitals. The quality of the teaching that these students receive therefore is highly variable. According to the latest figures available from ECFMG, only about 50% of IMGs including US IMGS find a residency spot through the National Matching Residency Program (NRMP) in the year that they apply. The IMGs who are not

US citizens have the option of returning to their country of origin and practice medicine, but the US citizens who attend offshore medical schools and don't find a residency, find themselves on a dead-end street. They have obtained the MD degree, but without the residency training, they are not able to practice Medicine. Many of them also carry a hefty student loan (200 -300 thousand dollars) which they will not be able to pay. To the best of my knowledge, no one has studied the fate of these medical graduates who cannot practice Medicine. Anecdotally, there are stories that some of these graduates are driving taxis or working in restaurants as waiters, but what happens to them as a group is largely unknown. We, the members of the Governing council of the IMG section of the AMA submitted a resolution to the house of delegates to study this, but it was not approved. What happens to their loan payments is also largely unknown. It was suggested by the house of delegates of AMA that this problem should be studied by the ECFMG, but to the best of my knowledge not much is going on at the ECFMG also regarding this issue.

Although, this anticipated shortage of physicians in the coming years is considered a national problem, not much is happening to alleviate this problem. There are well qualified and well-trained IMG physicians, who have completed residency training in their own countries, but are unable to enter the American medical work force, because they are required to complete the residencies all over again and there are not enough residency spots to accommodate them. It is apparent, that if these physicians could enter the medical work force, it would go a long way to solve the problem of physician shortage, but the American medical system is not ready to do that.

Recently, there has been a change in the graduation requirements for graduation from medical school and from the residencies. The graduation requirements are now competency based rather than time based. If there was a "competency test" that these IMG physicians could take to establish their competency, they should be eligible for a license to practice their specialty in the USA. However, no such test exists and to the best of my knowledge there are no plans to develop such an examination by the responsible agencies like the federation of

State boards for licensing, the American Board of Medical specialties, AAMC or AMA.

It seems possible to me that IMGs who have completed their residencies in their own countries should be allowed to take a test like that of Board certification (Or perhaps the board exam itself), and if they are competent, they would pass. However, even that does not seem possible because to take the Specialty exams given by American boards of Medical Specialties, one is required to complete a residency in the US approved by ACGME (Accreditation Council of Graduate Medical Education). It is a real "catch 22".

The argument offered for not allowing these otherwise medically qualified physicians is that they are not used to the American medical system, which seems to be a cogent argument.

However, one does not need to repeat a residency for 3 or 4 years to get used to the American medical system. A compromise of this situation seems to be that these physicians could do one year of residency to get used to the American medical system and take their subspecialty exam. If successful, they could practice their specialty. Although the IMG section has been pushing for such alternatives through the offices of AMA, they have not found much support for these ideas so far.

On the other hand, if a certain hospital or an institution needs a particular physician, they can petition the state board for a license. Some states will give licenses to certain physicians if they consider them "Experts". However, many of these "Experts" get a license to practice only in the institution that petitioned for them. Thus, they are held hostage to the institution and are unable to move to another institution, even though they may have opportunities to do so. Once again, the IMG section of the AMA proposed that such physicians, if they have worked for sufficient length of time (actual time yet to be determined) in one of the US hospitals, should be able to get an unrestricted license to practice Medicine, but that also has not happened so far.

From an academic standpoint also, it was time to start giving back. Again, to maintain the programs that I had created as the chief of the section of Endocrinology, it was appropriate to relinquish some responsibilities to the younger colleagues while I was still around so that I could nurture them and help them with the tasks that they were taking over.

As mentioned above, I had already stepped down as the Program Director in the year 2013 and the position of the Chief of the division of Endocrinology had already been advertised.

I, at this point, was actually helping to recruit a competent person who would take over the leadership and the section would continue to thrive. By this time, however, the chair that I had agreed with about this plan had left Michigan State University for another institution. Our new (acting) chair would not agree to the prior arrangement and she wanted me to work "full-time" and not the "academic year" that I was used to working for the last 4 years and would not even consider the possibility of me working 50% time as was agreed to by me and the previous chair. According to the university by-laws, since I was a tenured professor, with the agreement of a chair, we could develop any time schedule for me and that would be acceptable to the University. However, as mentioned above, the chair was being inflexible. One of the hallmarks of a good academic leader is that they put the welfare and progress of their unit, ahead of their own personal advancement. Perhaps, she thought that it was in the best interest of the department, that a person like me should work either fulltime or not at all. As a result of these discussions with the chair, it was apparent to me that if I wanted to continue the lifestyle that I had become used to, my best option would be to retire at this point. Consequently, I applied to retire. Since I was a tenured professor, the university by-laws would allow me to have a "consulting year" during which I would be working approximately half time. This would allow me to finish up any pending works that I had and would therefore allow for a smooth retirement.

At the time that I opted to retire, the medical school was embarking on a new curriculum called "shared discovery curriculum". One of the features of this curriculum was (is) that for the first two years the students will learn in small groups. They would be led by a faculty person called a fellow.

The students in each group will get to know each member of the group as well as the faculty person who would serve as their teacher, coach, and a mentor for the first two years of the medical school. The associate dean for education and the director of this new curriculum offered me a position as a faculty fellow and thereby I became one of the "founding faculty "for our new curriculum. I would continue to see patients one half day supervising fellows. This provided a very good transition, which is what I had originally asked the chair (roughly ½ time appointment), so I gladly accepted that.

I have done that for about three years now and this year, we have reduced it to about 10% teaching time and possibly one-half day of clinic. I will most likely continue to do this for about another year before fully retiring. I should add that I have enjoyed this arrangement.

25

SUMMARY AND CONCLUSIONS

Life is a journey. On this journey, we stop at a few stations. Although usually this journey is planned, destiny plays a major role as to how this journey turns out. In my case, for example, journey to the US, initially it was not even on my itinerary. When it did appear on the itinerary, it was expected to be of a short duration. The plan was to spend a few years (3 to 5) complete an Endocrinology fellowship and return to India. However, that did not happen.

The journey of life is hardly ever smooth. It comes with a few bumps, some minor and some not so minor. The loss of my spouse early in my career was a major bump that could have (and almost did), change the direction of this journey. I tried going back to India, to settle, but that did not happen, mostly because of my children.

The journey through the training years was rather smooth. Despite the warning by an older colleague that the road to academic medicine is long and tortuous, I managed to get into the track of academic medicine, and I believe thrived in it. I would say that the road to the entry into academic medicine may be difficult, but not tortuous. However, once you are on that road, the road to success in academic medicine can be long and tortuous. I have been fortunate to have navigated that road successfully but not without a few bumps. Those bumps have been in the form of events which lead one to think "Is this discrimination"? Based on one or two events, one would never know if this was truly a discrimination or not, but the thought crosses one's mind, that it is not fair. However, just like the journey of life comes with a few bumps, it is well known that "life is not fair". Has MSU been fair to me? I would say mostly "Yes!" but not entirely. Despite that, the journey has been a successful one from a professional standpoint. The question often pops up in my head "would it have been better or more successful, had I remained in India"? We would never know, but a reasonable expectation is that if I had joined AIIMS, at the end of my training as I had an opportunity to do so, that I would have risen to the rank of Professor, and thus the dream to become a professor would have been fulfilled. It is difficult to say if being a professor at AIIMS would have been better than being a professor at MSU. The former probably better, strictly from the Indian perspective, while being a professor at MSU appears to have been better from an International viewpoint. It has offered opportunities to remain connected with colleagues in India and many more opportunities to connect with international colleagues than a professorship in India might have. On the other hand, a professorship at AIIMS in India is held with much more esteem, at least in India than a professor ship at MSU in USA. In India a professor of Medicine is held at a level just a notch below God, whereas a professor in the USA at least in the eyes of the public is just another job although a highly respected one. It is the age-old question "Is it better to be big fish in a small pond or a small fish in big pond". The answer to this question, at least I will never know.

I believe that am not alone in rethinking this question. There are at least 25-30,000 Indian Physicians who immigrated here in the late 1960's and early 1970's. To get a better answer to this question, professor Vibha Bhalla of Bowling Green University, Bowling Green Ohio and I are conducting a survey among Indian physicians who have been here for more than 20 years on their perspective. We may know in a year or so if my colleagues have the same thoughts that I do or am I alone in this thinking process.

While the journey has been a successful one from the professional standpoint, how have we fared from the standpoint of the family?

There too, the journey has been a successful one. Our marriage of 40 years remains a happy one. We have three grown up children, who have matured into reasonably successful adults. Our daughter, an MBA, married to an MBA, has one son, who in his 8th grade is doing well academically and perhaps will have a successful career. My late, older brother used to say that the "success of a man is measured not by the success of his children, but his grandchildren". Perhaps I will not live long enough to see the success of my grandchildren, but I hope and wish that they will be equally successful, if not more than their parents, and I am around to see their success.

The two boys, one a physician and the other MBA, recently got married. They both opted to marry, local Caucasian women, presumably as a result of "falling in love". It is interesting to note that our older son got married in a remote island accompanied by his bride to be, without any friends or relatives, or parents from both sides of the family, whereas the younger one had a more traditional wedding ceremony, which included not only a Christian wedding but also an Hindu wedding ceremony.

So, for someone who did not even know about the "American dream" and arrived in this country with $8.00 in his pocket, has the "American dream" been achieved? If the success of achieving the American dream is measured by the professional success or the monetary success, then the answer is a resounding "Yes".

However, our personal, family, and social lives have changed in many ways because of migration to the US. The "Indian Community" is regarded as the "model community" in the USA. The first-generation immigrant members of this community are highly educated professionals, mostly engineers and doctors. Their children have been equally successful. Some of them have followed the path of their parents, while others have branched into other professions, like law, accounting, or business. We have every reason to be proud of our community.

We have been away from our large extended family for 50 years, and although the world has become smaller, due to the advancement of technology, the geographical distance does create a distance among relations. We have missed many happy occasions, such as weddings, birthday celebrations and sad occasions like a death in the family. Although both myself and my wife have remained well connected with our siblings, our children hardly know their aunts and uncles, and practically don't even know their cousins and they have quite a few of those. However, with the advent of technologies like Zoom, it has become a lot easier to remain in contact with the extended families back home. That seems to have made a noticeable difference as to how our children relate to their family in India now, as compared to a few years ago.

Some of the children don't speak the language of their parents (Mother tongue) which may be a disappointment for their parents. However, most of them understand the language that their parents speak. Moreover, there are many opportunities to learn a language if one has the desire to do so. Many universities including our own (Michigan State University) offer courses in several Indian languages. Our children took Hindi as a foreign language in college to improve their ability to speak, read and write this language. In addition, several religious organizations such as temples offer classes in Indian languages including Hindi and Sanskrit for free.

We now celebrate Christmas and Thanksgiving in addition to our own festivals like Diwali. It may appear that Christmas and Thanksgiving are celebrated with much more enthusiasm compared to Diwali. It is understandable, since the whole country is celebrating Christmas and Thanksgiving and it is easy to get into the flow of the celebrations, whereas only a small component, namely the Indian community is celebrating Diwali. However, Diwali is celebrated with equal enthusiasm by the Indian families at home and especially at the religious places like temples, where it is celebrated with prayers and the traditional fireworks. Many Indian families including our own decorate their houses with Diwali lights and candles and the younger generation does remember the night of Diwali and they also do something special like lighting candles and special food in their homes.

Most first-generation immigrants want to leave their traditions for the next generation to follow. One of the concerns we had was that many of our less well-known festivals and traditions will be forgotten but that does not appear to be the case. For example, the Custom of celebrating "Lohri " "Holi" and "Navaratri " are being kept alive mainly by the religious institutions. Our family has regularly celebrated Lohri at our temple for the last several years. We had a special celebration at the Lohri time when each of our grandsons were born. (Lohri is a special event if there is a newborn child, particularly a son in the family). It is interesting to note, that one of the neighbors specially came over to my son's house to invite our grandson to join in the celebration of Holi. He and his mother (She is a Caucasian woman) enjoyed the function thoroughly and say that they look forward to celebrating it every year. Many religious institutions also have "Sunday school "type classes where the younger generation can learn about epics like Mahabharata and Ramayana. Regular discussions are also held at these institutions about the teachings of Bhagwad Geeta for the benefit of children and adults alike. Hinduism and its traditions have survived for more than 5000 years in several countries and I am confident that it would survive in the USA as well, although, some traditions and the accompanying rituals may get modified.

We have learned about and observe the "Mother's Day" and the "Father's Day" regularly with our children. But we have not forgotten about the "Brother -sister day (Or Raksha Bandhan) and "Bhaiya Dooj" ."Raksha Bandhan" or "Rakhi", is a very important function and an Indian tradition signifying the bond between brothers and sisters. There are several stories that describe the origin of Raksha Bandhan. One of the legends is that Draupadi (A leading character from Mahabharata) saw the bleeding finger of Lord Krishna, tore a piece of her sari, and tied it to his finger to stop the bleeding. Moved by the gesture, Lord Krishna adopted her as his sister and vowed to protect her, which he did when the Kauravas tried to insult her by disrobing her in an open court. The legend has it that the Pandavas had lost everything in a gambling match with Duryodhana. As a result, he tried to publicly humiliate her by attempting to disrobe her.

In that effort, as he pulled her Sari, Lord Krishna by his miraculous powers kept adding to the length of her sari, such that Duryodhana could never pull her sari away from her. A poet described this episode by saying "Does this sari belong to this woman or is she made up of this sari" such that she could not be disrobed. Another legend is that this tradition was started hundreds of years ago in India when a Hindu Queen (Rani Karnavati) sent a piece of a sacred thread (Rakhi) to a Muslim King Humayun asking for his protection against the attack by the Sultan of Gujarat, Bahadur Shah. Greatly moved by this gesture, Humayun immediately sent his army for her protection. Since then, the tradition has been that sisters send the Rakhi to their brothers and in turn the brothers promise to "protect" their sister for as long as they live, which in modern times translates into the practice that the brothers frequently send gifts to their sisters.

For all the years that I have lived in the US my sisters would send me a" Rakhi" by mail and I would proudly wear it around my wrist. Friends and coworkers would ask if this was a "friendship bracelet" to which I would respond "No this is a bracelet to indicate the bond between brothers and sisters". I think most of them were appreciative of this tradition.

Similarly, "Bhaiya dooj" a festival celebrated usually two days after the Diwali festival is a day when the sisters wish their brothers a long and prosperous life and the brothers in turn promise to "protect" the sisters. According to the Hindu mythology, the day is celebrated to immortalize the day when the sister of Lord Krishna (Subhadra) showed her love for her brother. In the modern times, typically the sisters apply, a Tilak (a red mark) on the forehead of their brothers and wish them all the best. The brothers in turn provide some gifts to the sisters and promise to keep the bond strong forever.

Indian weddings are known to be large affairs with family and lots of friends getting together to celebrate. When Majumdar originally described in the stage of doubt, she implied that the parents would be concerned if their children would marry outside of their own community, but in many instances the opposite may be true. Since then, many interracial marriages have taken place. In several of the mixed marriages, the couples have decided to have more than one wedding ceremony. We attended a wedding where three different marriage ceremonies were performed. First, a Sikh wedding (The father of the groom was a Sikh), followed by a Nikah or a Muslim wedding (The father of the bride was a Muslim) and finally a Jewish wedding (The mother of the bride was a Jewish woman). However, sometimes, the wedding ceremonies are now celebrated as "Destination weddings" "with very few family members and sometimes none, which may be a disappointment for some parents. If an inter-racial marriage is successful, the couple can learn about the customs, traditions, and rituals of each other and thus their lives are enriched. They can go on and adopt what they like about each other's customs. In the process, however, some of the traditions from each of the religions (Hindu, Catholic, Jewish or others) may be dropped. This may be a cause of concern for some parents.

While the loss of some of these traditions may be disappointing to the first generation of immigrants, it is not entirely unexpected. When two cultures merge, in the process of acculturation, some traditions are dropped, and some new ones are acquired from the adopted culture. Moreover, the loss of these traditions affects only the first generation of immigrants. The children of the first generation of immigrants do not (and will not) miss them because they were not aware of it in the first place. Hopefully, they would continue to live happily in their adopted culture which is a mixture of what their parents brought with them and those that they acquired on their own in their adopted land.

Life is not a balance sheet where one can add the pluses and minuses and come up with a net balance. Regardless of what the balance may be, I derive strength from our holy scriptures "Bhagwad Geeta", which essentially says:

Whatever happened: Happened for the best.
Whatever will happen: Will happen for the best.
Whatever is happening: Is happening for the best.
What did you lose, for which you are crying?
What did you bring with you that has been lost?
What did you produce, that has been destroyed?

Whatever you have, you got from here.
Whatever you have given, was given here.
What is yours today, belonged to someone else yesterday and will belong to someone else tomorrow.
Change is the law of universe. So, live with it.

Consequently, we are living in our present environment, happily with all the changes that the time and the location has brought.

The End.

REFERENCES

1. Jaswant Singh, in Jinnah ,India-partition, independence.2009 (Publisher Rupa and Co.).

2. Mary Sanchez (Kansas star columnist) – Published in Lansing State Journal. Nov 26,2014. Page A6.

3. Christina Ilie. The acculturation of immigrants case study; types of acculturation of the Romanian immigrants in Madrid ". International Journal of business and social research (IJBSR). 2013;3:84-88.

4. Majumdar U. A view and review of the South Asian Woman's Immigrant experience .Journal of South Asian Literature. 1986;XXI (1) 47-53

5. Torrey EF, and TaylorRL – Cheap labor from poor nations. AM J Psych. 1973;130:428-433

6. Derbyshire RC. Warm bodies in white coats. JAMA 1975;232(10)1034-1035

7. Weiss RJ, Kleinman J, Brandt UC et al .The effect of Importing physicians. Return to the pre-Flexnerian standard. New Eng J Med. 1974;290:1453-1458

8. Saywell RM, Studnicki J, Bean JA, Ludke RL. A performance comparison: USMGs-FMGs house staff physician. Am J Pub Health 1980;70:23-28

9. Ibid. A performance comparison:USMGs-FMGs attending Physicians. Am J Pub Health. 1979;69:57-62

10. Mick S, Comfort M. The quality of care of international medical graduates: How does it compare to that of U.S. medical graduates? Medical Care Res Review. 1997; 54:379-413.

11. Bhalla V. "We wanted to end disparities at work": Physician migration, racialization and a struggle for equality. J of American Ethnic History2010;29: (3) 1-77

12. Bharat S Shah. Problems of foreign medical graduates: India Abroad June 6,1975).

13. Desbiens NA, Vidallet HJ Jr. Discrimination against international medical graduates in the United States residency program selection process. BMC Med Educ 10, 5 (2010). https://doi. org/10.1186/1472-6920-10-5 -10-5).

14. Tsugawa Y, Jena AB, Newhouse RL, Orav EJ, Jha AK, et al. Quality of care delivered by general Internists in US hospitals who graduated from foreign Vs US medical schools: Observational study. BMJ 2017;356: j273.

15. IMG Member Alert [reply-119753@hq.ama-assn.org] Sent: Wednesday, August 07, 2013)

16. GME funding :4 things students should know about new GME bill. AMA newsletter May 20,2015.

17. (International Medical graduates in American medicine a position paper by the IMG section governing council. 2013)

18. Nwadiuko J, Varadaraj V, Ranjit A, International Medical Graduates – A critical component of the Global Health Force. JAMA 2018;319 765-766.).

19. https://www.ndtv.com/india-news/ndtv-mid-term-poll-does-india-still-want-arranged-marriages-498043)

20. Modern lessons from arranged marriages J. Hyun Lee – New York Times, published Jan 18, 2013.

21. Onishi N "divorce in south Korea: striking a new attitude. New York times 9/21/2003

22. https://www.indiatoday.in/education-today/gk-current-affairs/story/india-has-the-lowest-divorce-rate-in-the-world-1392407-2018-11-20

23. EpsteinR, Pandit M, Thakar M. How love emerges in arranged marriages: Two cross cultural studies .J Comparative family studies. 2013;44:341-360

24. Copen CF, Daniels K, and Mosher WD. National Health Statistics Reports No. 64, April 4, 2013 (US Department of Health and Human Services Center for Disease Control and Prevention. National Center for Health Statistics).

25. Manning WD, Cohen J. Premarital cohabitation and marital dissolution: An examination of recent marriages Journal of Marriage and Family. 2012; 74:377-387.

26. Dush CMK, Cohan C, Amato PR. The relationship between cohabitation and marital quality and stability: change across cohorts. Journal of Marriage and Family. 2003; 65:539-540.

27. Elisabeth Kubler Ross. M.D. On death and dying Simon and Schuster publishers

28. (https://timesofindia.indiatimes.com/life-style/health-fitness/health-news/the-scientific-reason-behind-the-mundan-ceremony/articleshow/67072737.cms.

29. https://www.theguardian.com/lifeandstyle/2013/jul/12/should-young-children-go-to-funerals

30. AARP magazine June/July 2015 "Are you real" and letters to editor. AARP Aug/Sept 2015 issue.

31. PalepuA, Carr P Freidman RH et al. Minority faculty and academic rank in Medicine. JAMA. 1998; 280:767-771.

32. Peterson NB, FreidmanRH, Ash AS. Faculty self-reported experience with racial and ethnic discrimination in academic medicine. J Gen Int Med. 2004; 19:259-265

33. Eligon, J and Smith M Emergency declared in Ferguson after shooting. New York times. Aug 10,2015

34. Horowitz J, Corasaniti N and Southhall A. Nine killed in shooting at black church in Charleston. New York times June 17,2015.

35. Derrick Bryson Taylor. George Floyd Protests; a timeline New York times June 2,2020

36. Published in The Villages Daily Sun, Feb 17, 2020 page A18)

37. Nicholas Kristoff. The Asian advantage. New York Times digest. Oct 11,2015.

ACKNOWLEDGEMENTS

An old African proverb says, "it takes a village to raise a child". My life may not be an exception to that rule, and therefore, I have many people to thank. First and foremost, I want to thank my parents (Both deceased now) especially my father, who always emphasized the importance of education. It was that emphasis that drove me to enter medical school. Secondly, I want to thank my three older brothers for their moral and financial support, without which I would not have become a physician. The faculties of medical college Amritsar made sure that I became a good doctor, the faculties of the All-India Institute of Medical Sciences made sure that I became a good Internist and the faculties of the University of Cincinnati and the Medical College of Wisconsin made sure that I became a good Endocrinologist. I am immensely thankful to all those faculty members who have contributed to my becoming a successful endocrinologist. Almost all my academic life was spent at the Michigan State University and I am immensely thankful to several hundred students, residents, fellows, and the faculty colleagues, without whom I would not have achieved academic success.

As for this book, the stimulus to write this book was my late wife (Veena) and the book is dedicated to her. I wanted to share with you all, the emotional roller coaster that we went through during her illness and eventual passing, but more importantly to emphasize that it is possible to put life back together even after such a disastrous event. I am thankful to my secretary Jinie Shirey who very patiently typed the first draft of this book nearly 5 years ago. I am immensely thankful to my present wife (Ramma) and my children who endured the long working hours that I put in while I was working full time. Throughout that time, and even in retirement , while I was busy with other assignments including writing this book , she almost singlehandedly kept our family life running smoothly and never complained. Finally, I am thankful to the staff at the Global summit publishing house, particularly Madison Barnes and Alister Quill, who have been instrumental in getting this book see the light of the day.

www.ingramcontent.com/pod-product-compliance
Lightning Source LLC
LaVergne TN
LVHW040144080526
838202LV00042B/3018